The Mysterious Stranger

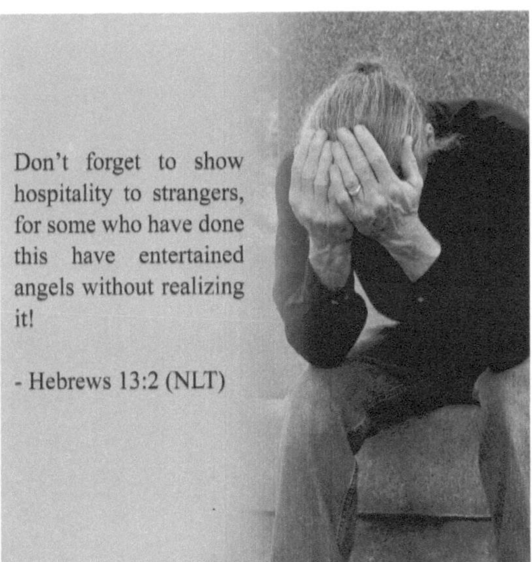

JOHN MARINELLI

TABLE OF CONTENTS

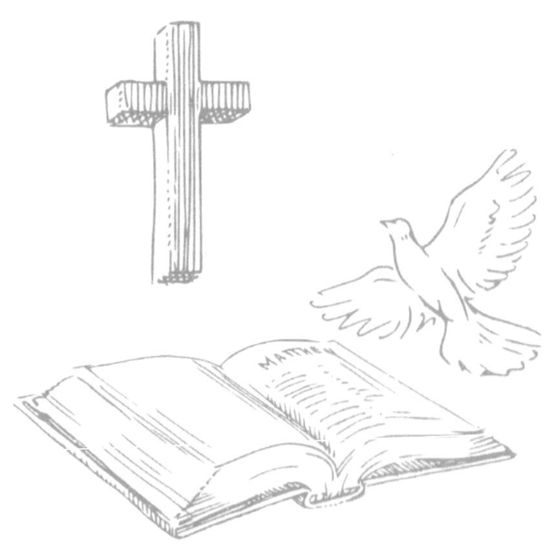

PREFACE

The Mysterious Stranger is a Christian fiction story. Although the story is fiction, the basis for the story is not. It was inspired by a Bible text that makes reference to human beings entertaining angels without realizing it.

> (Do not be forgetful of hospitality, for through this, some have **entertained angels** unawares. New American Standard Bible) Hebrews 13:2

The storyline will follow Jim Smith, a mild mannered reporter with the Christian Gazette, a national newspaper, which focuses on Christian events, people and happenings around the world.

Jim, our reporter, takes an assignment to track down a mysterious stranger that keeps showing up in different places at different times in the lives of different folks that need help in some way.

The people Jim scheduled for an interview had one common thread that bound them all together. They all encountered a mysterious stranger that helped them in their time of need.

The story will address some modern day social issues and will also touch on God's Will, Man's Destiny, Faith, Loyalty, Free Will and The Authority of The Bible.

The reader will accompany our reporter as he talks to eyewitnesses to an encounter with a stranger that just happened to show up at the point of their need.

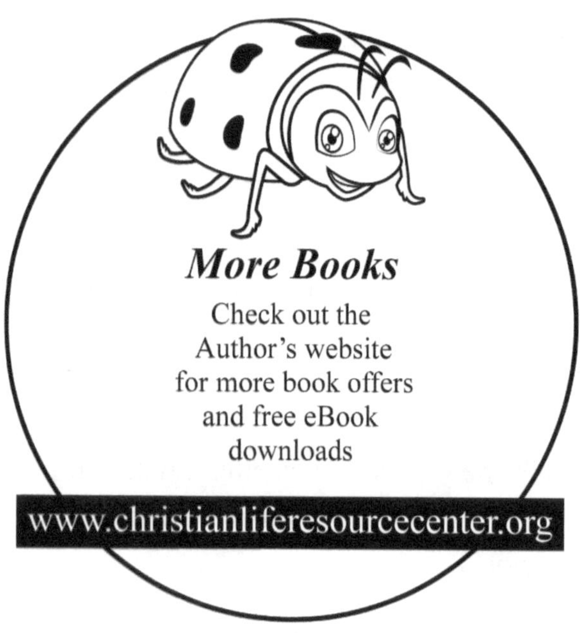

INTRODUCTION

Our story begins in the summer of 2010 at the home of Joe Jenkins. It's Joe's 85th birthday celebration. Joe was a WWII survivor of the Battle of Normandy. He came home wounded along with many other army veterans.

Joe was the first interview on Jim's list as he searched for the mysterious stranger. They sat together on Joe's "Wrap-A-Round" porch with a cup of coffee.

Joe was reluctant to talk about the encounter because it was during WWII at a time when he experienced a lot of trauma and horrible scenes of dying men that still haunted him in his dreams. However, he agreed when the rest of the family also encouraged him to talk about the stranger and his part in the D-Day invasion.

Jim began asking Joe some questions, trying to get him to cut to the chase. "When and where did you first meet this stranger?" Was he in a military uniform? What did he say to you? What did he look like? "Go ahead, Mr. Jenkins. Give us all the details." This is how he remembered it, in his own words.

It was 1943 and the United States was up to its elbows in WW II. By November, gasoline, bicycles, footwear, silk, nylon, fuel oil, stoves, meat, lard, shortening, margarine, processed foods, dried fruits, canned milk, firewood and coal, jams, jellies and butter would all be rationed. The United States was at war with Japan, Germany and other Nazi led forces.

Women went to work to fill the vacancies of men that went to war. Many factories stopped making consumer goods and retooled for the production of tanks, airplanes, guns and ammunition.

Young men were joining the military as volunteers. Bill Anderson, my best friend and I were no exception. We were typical of 1943 American youth. We were patriotic and ready and willing to defend our nation from the tyranny of Nazism. We would never ever think of burning the national flag like some young people do today. We had respect for the flag and the country it represented.

It was hard for us to imagine being combat ready soldiers. We never even got in a fight after school. I guess you would say that we were popular and liked by everyone. Armed conflict and killing was not in our vocabulary. We both felt deeply about protecting our country and way of life. The thinking back in 1943 was, "If we don't fight, who will?"

Jim spoke up and said, "What does Bill have to with your encounter with an angel?"

"A lot", said Joe. "Bill was there when the stranger showed up."

We talked a lot about being soldiers. We never though once about getting killed or even wounded. That stuff always happened to the other guy, which we didn't know personally.

For a people who are free, and who mean to remain so,
a well-organized and armed militia is their best
security.

Thomas Jefferson

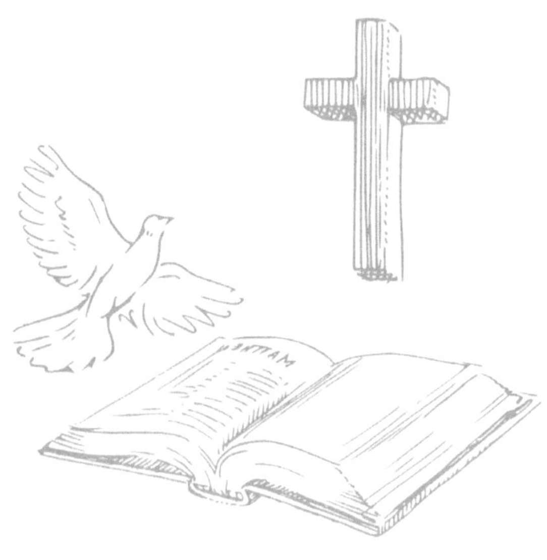

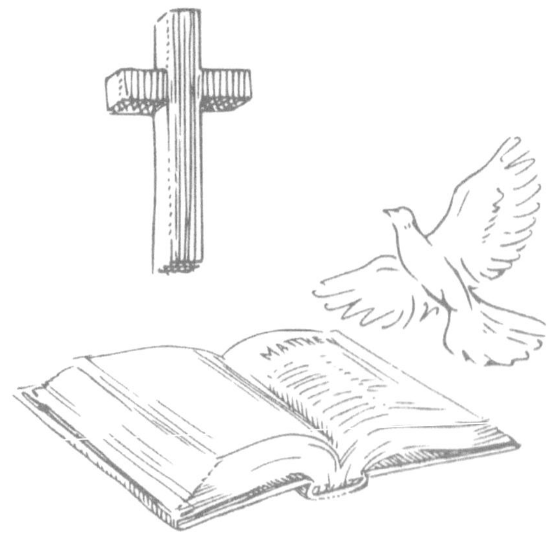

CHAPTER ONE

JOINING UP, BCT AND DEPLOYMENT

Bill and I remembered what the army recruiter said about enlisting and being drafted. On September 16, 1940, the United States instituted the Selective Training and Service Act, which required all men between the ages of 21 - 45 to register for the draft. This was the first peacetime draft in United States' history.

During WWII, the army accepted recruits at 16 but those soldiers could not be deployed to the front lines until age 18. We knew that we needed to wait until our 18th birthday to enlist so we could go to the front lines and fight. But that was only a few months away for Bill and less for me.

We enlisted under the "buddy" system. I pushed Bill to join up while we were still in school. I said, why couldn't we go right away? If we did, it would keep my dad from hounding me about college. I didn't want to go to college right out of high school. It would be as if I were hiding from my responsibility to defend our flag and great country. I was proud of being an American and wanted to invest my time as a soldier to insure that we would still be free.

Freedom was important to all of us. We knew that those that came before us paid for our freedom with the blood of their sons and family members. It wasn't like today. No one burned the flag or even thought of badmouthing our country. We were proud of our heritage and were willing to die if necessary so our families can live in freedom.

There was too much at stake to sit in a college learning about Plato and ancient history. The war was far more interesting. After all, Bill and I played Cowboys and Indians and even WAR with our friends when we were little. It all seemed like another game to play but this time as grown ups.

The army wanted to know if we were smart or not. They tested us for being crazy, stupid, quick-tempered and a bunch of other things.

Well, we passed with flying colors. Bill did a little better than I did but we both made it. They even did background checks on us to see if we had any criminal records. If we did, they would have rejected us right then and there. They also did an FBI investigation into our habits and loyalties to see if we were ever involved with communism, secret societies or coloration with the "Third Reich." That is what we called Nazism.

I guess the army wanted to be sure that we were loyal

Americans and willing to fight for "Old Glory." Just so you all know, "Old Glory" is a reference to the Flag. Men have fought in wars since the 1700 under its banner, defending their right to be free and to govern themselves.

Basic Combat Training (BCT) is basic training or boot camp for civilians who want to join the military. It turns civilians into soldiers. We learned to march and shoot a rifle. They taught us survival skills and prepared us for life in the army. It was an intense 10 weeks.

We finally finished BCT and went on for another 3-weeks of advanced combat training where we learned hand-to-hand combat, how to gather and use intelligence, war strategies and more survival skills.

Three days later we received our deployment papers. We were to report to the Norfolk Naval Base, Norfolk, VA. It was the world's biggest naval base at that time. That's where the troop transport ships were docked.

The army decided to fly Bill and I to London England from Norfolk with other special forces instead of going by ship. Upon arrival in England we were assigned to set up last minute training exercises.

We did not know exactly what type of mission we were to go on but it was evident that it was important. We kept seeing new faces and meeting new soldiers from the 1st and 29th army divisions. They arrived by the busload. Everyone felt that there was something big about to happen but we would not even try to guess what.

The next day, we got orders to board the troop ships that would transport the invasion force. It was time to see if Bill's dream would come true or not. Would he be one of the thousands that died on the beaches of Normandy?

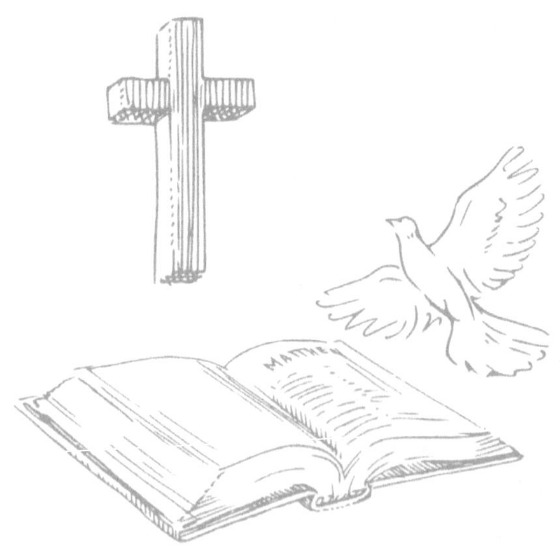

CHAPTER TWO

ZERO HOUR AND THE MYSTERIOUS STRANGER

Zero hour finally arrived and the Invasion of Normandy had begun. It was 4:55 A. M. on June 6th 1944. Over 100,000 Allied troops made it to shore that day. But it was just beginning for Bill and me. We were off loaded from the transport ship into a landing craft. Other ships were doing the same with their soldiers.

As we crowded into the landing craft, I looked at Bill and said, " Well, here we go. Good luck my friend. God be with us both in our hour of despair." Bill agreed saying, "Lord help us."

After 30 minutes or so, there were hundreds of landing crafts circling the area. Many had already landed on the beaches of Normandy. Bill and I were headed towards Omaha Beach. The seas were up with high winds and waves. The temperature was around 59 degrees.

I said to myself… "Get it together man." Then I cried out

to God in my heart saying, "I don't want to die here, I don't want to die."

Nothing went as planned. In the predawn darkness, the crafts carrying the invasion force took longer than expected to form up, and many hit the beach without armor protection. The various waves of landing crafts became mixed up in the confusion.

Every landing craft was taking on water. Some of the landing crafts began sinking. Those that stayed afloat took enemy fire. Landing crafts were being hit by enemy shells and exploding. Most of the men succumbed to seasickness.

As our landing craft approached the beach it hit a floating mine, about 300 yards from the seashore. Bill and I were tossed overboard into a rough sea and a barrage of enemy machinegun fire. We sank to the bottom right away because of the weight of our packs. We struggled for a while and then used our utility knives to cut loose and surfaced, only to hear bullets flying everywhere. There was nowhere to go and the water was too deep for us to stand up.

After a few minutes of treading water, we hitched a ride from another landing craft by hanging on for dear life. We moved closer to Omaha Beach.

The only thing we could do is play dead in the water letting the tide bring us into shore. We had already seen other soldiers lift their heads or try to stand up and were immediately shot by enemy snipers.

Then Bill called to me saying, "Come on Joe, let's run for cover near those rocks." In the midst of enemy fire, we ran for our lives as bullets whistled in the air all around us.

It was there in that moment that Bill and I both saw a mysterious stranger on the battlefield. He was dressed in all white and kept getting in our way. It looked to me like he was actually catching the enemy's bullets. We were in the direct line of fire as snipers and machinegun nests honed in on us, yet we were not hit.

This mystery man motioned for us to follow him and we did. He led us to a place of safety. Then he dashed back into the line of fire to help other commandos. We didn't see him again on the beach.

"Thank God? I said to Bill. Did you see that man? Bill said, "You mean the man in white?" I said, "Yeah" We both gave glory to God and knew it was the hand of God that was upon us. I felt invincible. I don't know what Bill felt but I was ready to fight the enemy, knowing I was not going to be hurt. I remembered that scripture that said something like this, If God be for us, who can be against us?

"We are safe for the moment." I looked over at Bill again and said, "Where is the rest of our division?" Bill said, "Who knows? We'll probably see them later today."

Then I looked back over Omaha beach and saw it full of fallen comrades from 20-feet seaward of the water's edge inward as far as the tide had carried them. I knew then within my heart that I was looking at most of our division. We were the lucky ones. So far, we had survived. We could say with confidence that if it hadn't been for God, …you fill in the rest.

Finally we reached the 1st of many hedgerows. We stopped to survey the area when we met 20 or so U.S. Army Infantrymen. As we talked and greeted each other, out of nowhere, the enemy launched a surprise attack and Bill was killed in action by an exploding mortar. I was badly wounded and almost died myself. If it hadn't been for the angel that showed up out of nowhere, I would have died. He rushed me to a nearby field hospital.

Jim spoke up saying, "Wait a minute. How did you know he was the angel?

Joe replied, "Because before I passed out from the shock of being wounded, I saw that he was dressed all in white and my blood was not staining his clothing, not a drop stayed on him. He rushed me straight into a field hospital and then vanished. The folks in the hospital tent found me on the floor but didn't know how I got there because there was no one with me.

Two other army guys were killed and four were severely wounded. I woke up a week later in that field hospital only to learn that Bill had been killed. My injuries were serious but not life threatening.

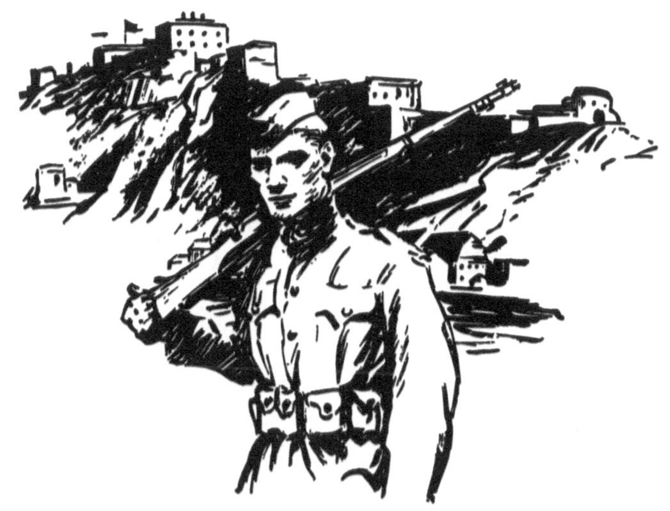

"For we wrestle not against flesh and blood, but against principalities, against powers, against the rulers of the darkness of this world, against spiritual wickedness in high *places*." Ephesians 6:12

CHAPTER THREE

LIFE, DEATH AND AGAIN

I was really bad off, not physically but emotionally. I just couldn't deal with Bill's death. Why did the angel save us on the beach if Bill was to die later? What difference did it make when and where he would be killed? Why was I spared and he was not? After all, I was single but Bill had a wife back home that was pregnant with his son. My dreams were not yet even dreamed. I had no idea what I'd be doing and where I'd be after the war but Bill's dream and destiny were already launched. He was going somewhere. It just didn't make since.

I suffered with guilt and depression for years. I couldn't help but think that it should have been me instead of Bill that died that day on the battlefield. My self-esteem was lower than low. I was worthless in my own eyes. I became suicidal, thinking I had no reason to go on in life. God must have made a mistake. Bill should be living, not me.

As you can imagine, I started to drink and became an alcoholic. Then I became homeless because I couldn't keep myself together enough to have a job.

The years slowly went by with me thinking that the angel made a mistake when he led Bill and me to safety and shielded me from the mortar attack. I was angry with this mystery man because he let Bill die and me live.

If it weren't for God, I would have ended my life long ago. Somehow, by the grace of God, I learned to live again. Maybe it was that scripture I read in the Bible. It said,

"For God so loved the world, that he gave his only begotten Son, that whosoever believeth in him should not perish, but have everlasting life." *John 3:16*

After reading the scripture, I realize that God was not punishing me. He actually loved me and wanted me to live forever with Him. I believed in Jesus, God's only Son and became a, "Whosoever."

Bill may have been lost in WWII but not forgotten. He was in God's hands and I knew I'd see him again in the hereafter. Little did I know then that the, "Hereafter" would show up a few years down the road.

Jim interrupted Joe saying, "What do you mean?"

Joe explained, you see, Bill didn't really die. The army got the wrong guy. The angel also saved Bill. He took the brunt of the mortar blast and shielded Bill.

Bill was seriously injured but lived to see another day.

Jim responded, "Tell us all about it"

Joe answered Jim, "I don't think so. That story is Bill's to tell, not mine."

So Jim Moves on to the next person on his interview list.

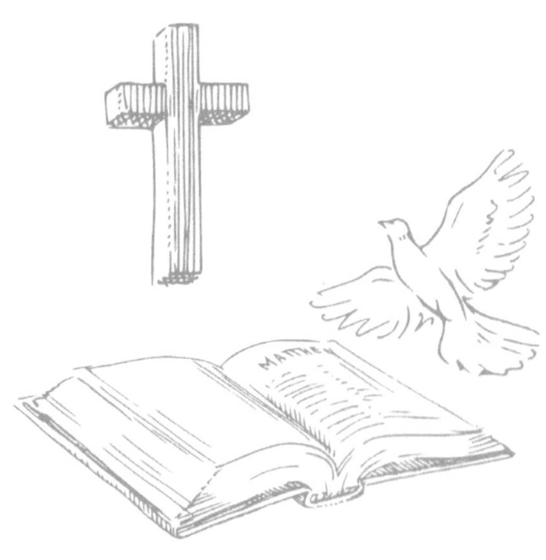

Chapter Four

Bill Junior And The Stranger

Jim was given Bill Junior's name and phone number and suggested that he interview him. He was the son of Joe's best friend and war hero. He also had and encounter with the mysterious stranger. So Jim set out for his next story in hopes of tracking down the mysterious stranger.

Bill Jr. agreed to meet with Jim and they sat down one Sunday afternoon over a cup of coffee. Jim wanted to know all about the mysterious stranger.

Bill Jr. began to share his story. "I was minding my own business in Alaska when I was called up for military duty as part of the build up of the Vietnam conflict."

The draft took me and sent me directly to a naval boot camp. They said that the Army and Marines had already met their quotas for that month and the other services were not recruiting at that time."

So Bill Jr. ended up in the naval boot camp at Great Lakes

IL. Twelve weeks of exercise, running, school and discipline whipped him into shape both mentally and physically. He was now ready to face the world but not before his two year draft was up.

Bill Jr. was assigned to a destroyer out of San Diego, CA. that was headed for Vietnam. Their assignment was to support marine forces with off shore bombardments north of Saigon. It was a joint exercise with SEATO forces. The joint effort was to take place in the South China Sea.

So there he was in the middle of the ocean with Australian and English war ships playing war until a junior officer of the deck wrongly read and execute order to change course. The officer turned to the left instead of right as the command dictated. The two ships collided in a matter of minutes. The USS Frank E. Evans moved directly across the bow of the HMAS Melbourne of the Royal Australian Navy. It was a light air craft carrier.

The Evans was cut in half, with the Bow half sinking in about 2 minutes taking 74 men to a watery grave. There were probably close to 200 survivors either in the water or on the aft section of the ship, which stayed afloat. There were no casualties on Melbourne. It was probably the worst navel sea disaster in modern times.

Bill Jr. was able to save the lives of two of my shipmates by pulling them from the twisted metal of the impacted area of the ship. All three men ended up in the sea with many other sailors. Bill Jr. made sure they all had life jackets.

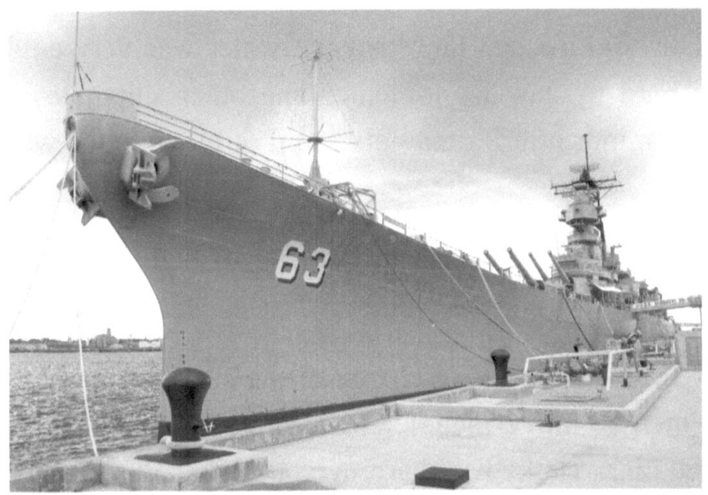

Bill Jr. explains, "The three of us along with many other survivors were left to tread water for many hours until we were rescued. Among the 74 men lost were three brothers that requested assignment together. This was the 1st time the navy allowed the same duty to relatives since the seven Sullivans died in WW II.

"I kept telling my friends that God would work everything out for good." One of the men commented saying, "How can you say that with such assurance"

Bill Jr. Responds, "I said it was because my mother believed the Bible and she said that was what it said would happen."

Bill Jr. went from being an agnostic in the wilderness of

Alaska to a believer in the God of his parents. The fact remained; they were still treading water, watching for sharks and rescue ships.

Bill Jr. told his dad later that the water was very cold. It was hard to stay cognoscente. The other shipmates sustained minor injuries that left a trail of blood in the water.

The HMAS Melbourne of the Royal Australian Navy was badly damaged and had drifted out of sight. It was just after 3:00 AM under a cloudy darkened sky.

Bill Jr. decided to take charge of the situation and forced the men to move their legs and arms to keep the blood circulating. He kept a sharp eye out for sharks that might be attracted to the blood in the water. The men had no life raft, and had to share life jackets.

The situation grew worst as the sun rose above the China Sea. The sea began to form white caps and large rolling waves. The sky poured out its thunder and rain. The winds blew as though there was no tomorrow. The survivors of the collision were growing weaker with every hour that passed.

Bill Jr. was at the end of days or so he thought. It would have been easy to just give up and drown but Bill Jr. would not. He, instead, called on God to help him. He remembered what his dad told him before he left home.

Bill Sr. told him, "Son, if you ever get into a jam, where you feel you cannot get out of by your own power, call upon the Lord. He is a very present help in times of trouble."

It was in that moment, when Bill Jr. was about to die, that his parents' faith became his. He called upon the Lord and trusted in God to save him and his shipmates.

Suddenly, several sharks began to circle the men in the sea. Bill Jr. put it this way, "I saw many big sharks circling us but I also saw another survivor or someone anyway in the sea with us. He radiated light in every direction that brought heat to us and kept the sharks a bay.

Jim asked for more details, "What was this man wearing? Where did he get the light? How long did it last?

Bill Jr. told him that he wasn't sure. All he knew was that the frigid sea became like a warm bath and the light directed the rescue ships to know where we were.

Finally, after many hours in the China Sea, they all were rescued and placed upon various other ships for treatment or observation.

Bill Jr. started showing signs of P.T.S.D. (Post Traumatic Stress Disorder) The navy sent him back stateside to spend some time with his parents. Bill Jr. had to fight one more battle to regain his peace of mind. His emotional state would keep him from any further military service.

CHAPTER FIVE

THE GRIZZLY AND THE WIFE

"So", Jim moves along in search of the mysterious stranger. He finally catches up with Bill Sr. They agree to meet and discuss Bill Jr. as well as his encounter with the mystery man.

Jim, being polite asked Bill Sr. "How's Bill Jr.?" Bill Sr. spoke up to answer the question.

"My son, the bum…lost in the wilderness of Alaska again. You'd think he'd call or write once in a while. However he did call us about six months ago. We talked for almost an hour, at my expense. You know that he was a wilderness guide before Vietnam. Yeah, he took people on guided adventures into the Alaskan Bush. Now he just traps, grows his own food and hunts."

"He is living as though it was the 18th century with no electric, no neighbors except for a few Indians and no real job and very little income.

He barters for things and sells his furs or extra crops if the growing season is good. It's a rough life and he loves it?"

Jim asked Bill, "What about his wife? We know nothing of her?"

Bill Sr. looks at Jim and says, "She's another story. They met at a karaoke bar and hit it off right away. Apparently she can sing, among other things. She is around 5' 1', shapely, brown hair, green eyes with tattoos all over her arms and legs. She goes by the name, "Toni." Ain't that a kick in the head? She has a boy's name but with an "I" instead of a "Y" at the end. Bill Jr. said she was from the Bronx, NY where all the tough gals live."

"Well, she's a pretty little thing and tough as nails. Bill Jr. says she chops wood, handles the garden, cooks most of the meals, and even hunts with him. They are a perfect couple, both nuts."

"Bill Jr. had to tell me how Toni saved him from a Grizzly. He first had to give me all the statistics on this kind of bear. He said, "There are currently about 55,000 wild grizzly bears located throughout North America, most of which reside in Alaska.""

"Bill and Toni were hunting and a grizzly came into their camp and attacked Bill Jr. before he could get to his rifle. Toni was already up because it was near sunrise and she was cooking. The smell of food must have drawn the grizzly near."

"Well Bill Jr. ran and as he ran he yelled for Toni. The bear roared and stood straight up. He was over six and a half feet and looked to be about 650 pounds. As the bear came down he swatted at Bill Jr. with his paw and lunged forward towards him."

"Toni grabbed Bill Jr.'s rifle and fired off two shots at the bear. She did not aim to hit the bear, only to scare it away and she did. Bill Jr. saw the grizzly run away."

Bill Sr. continues, "The Alaskan Bush is a wild place. Life is hard and few make it that come from the lower 48. Bill Jr. is one of the exceptions."

"Their homestead is in the interior close to Fairbanks with temperatures that dip into the minus 50-degree range. Storms snow them in frequently. Winter power outages come with the territory. Winter is a solid five months out of the year."

"The mid-summer weather is usually nice, in the 70s. The sunsets briefly around midnight but the skies never truly darken. However, the reverse is true for winter months. Folks live in the dark every day."

"The cost of living is definitely higher and is even worse as you go deeper into the more remote areas. The state has a very laid-back feel to it. I guess that's why Bill Jr. likes it so much."

"The bush of Alaska is definitely a different lifestyle. It is nothing like the cities in the lower 48 states. It is truly a "Last Frontier State."

"Bill Jr. has spent the better part of 3-years building a homestead. He has solar heat, underground coolers to store food and perishable supplies and a natural freezer in winter right at his door. He now owns 50 acres of shear wilderness full of snakes, bears, fox, wolves, and rabbits, birds of all kinds and even deer and moose. His closest neighbor is an hour and a half by snow mobile."

"The fishing is great with Salmon, Trout, Northern Pike and a lot more. They even have a special storage place to salt and store fish for the winter."

"It's not a lifestyle that Sarah and me would desire. It's too cold, too far from civilization and too expensive to live. We'll leave that up to Bill Jr. and Toni."

Jim again interrupts saying to Bill, " Joe told us that you also had an encounter with this mysterious stranger. How about sharing it with us?"

Bill responded to Jim by saying, "Not today. We are just about to go off for a 2-week vacation in Florida. Give me your card and I'll call you when we get back."

Jim makes a mental note for his sequel article thinking, "The teenage romance that blossomed into love only to be cut off by war still burned in Sarah's heart. Although she felt sorrow and suffered from the effects of war and trag-edy, she was able to forge ahead towards whatever destiny awaited her. She knew that God would work everything together for her good because she loved Him and was called according to His purposes."

Bill Sr. makes a final comment saying, "Life is all about perspective. We stand or fall on how we see things. Some can laugh and others cry over the same experience. Sometimes we laugh and cry but those that live life with joy and peace, trust in God to work it all together for their good." (Romans 8:28)

> "Trust in the LORD with all your heart and lean not on your own understanding; in all your ways acknowledge him, and he will make your paths straight." **Proverbs 3:5-6**

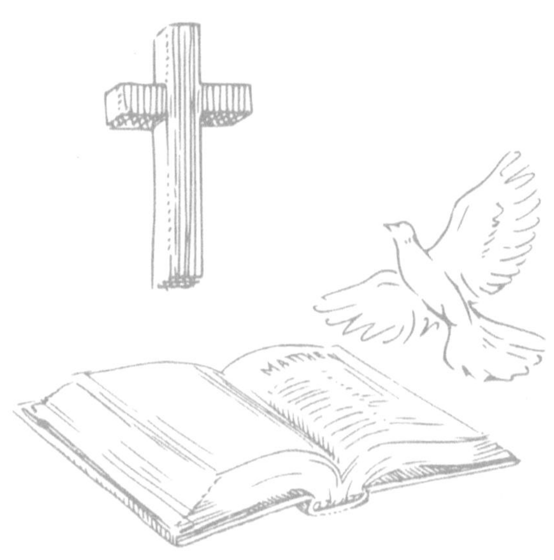

Chapter Six

The 600-Mile Bus Ride

Three days have passed since Jim interviewed Bill Sr. and now he is on his way to meet a bus driver that supposedly had an angelic encounter. Jim will hear, first hand, how the Mysterious Stranger touched the lives of the bus driver and some of his passengers.

Jim drove a hundred miles north to meet with the bus driver in Plant City, FL. They had made an appointment the day before.

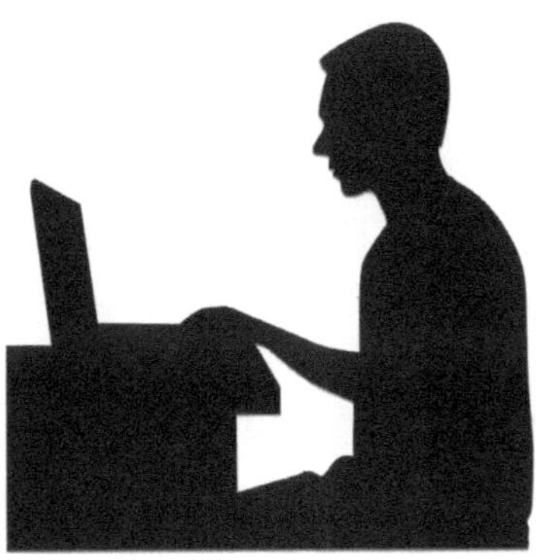

As they both sat at the counter of a nearby restaurant, they were served a coup of coffee and a Danish. Jim asked the bus driver to share with him the encounter.

Time had passed over since the "Mysterious Stranger" came to town but the events that took place were not forgotten.

The bus driver began to share saying, "I can still remember the sunset and the rippling of the water as the wind blew across the lake. I can also remember that awful night when it rained so hard that mudslides took half of our mountain road. *This is where it all began.*"

"The bus I was to drive was late the night he arrived. It was after three A.M. There was a lot of fog and few people at the bus station. But I was there because I was the bus driver. I had 600 miles of open road to observe this man. I even talked with him for about a hundred miles."

"He never told us his name. His dress was subdued and pretty much ordinary. He was a tall, dark and somewhat handsome man with broad shoulders. He was soft spoke and his voice comforting. His bearded face made him look tough like a truck driver but when he spoke, you knew he was a gentle man."

"He quickly became everybody's friend and yet nobody really knew him. Folks painted a portrait of what they wanted to see. They seem to project their mental image on to him. Who he really was, was mine alone to know. For some unknown reason he allowed me, a bus driver, to see him as he really was."

"He got on my bus at the beginning of the line and traveled with me to the end of the line. We talked about a lot of things from the weather to the future."

"His kindness and soft-spoken nature made it easy for me to share things about myself that I had long since forgotten. It was as though I was being "X-Rayed" and those sad and hurtful feeling from yesteryear just dissolved away as we discussed them. Time itself seemed to stop; yet I know that didn't happen."

"He left the bus with a young couple that just got married and they all entered the bus station. He had no carryon luggage or suitcases, just himself."

"I checked in and turned over my keys to the station manager and then looked for the stranger to say goodbye but he was nowhere to be found. The young couple told me that they turned their back to him to find a seat and when they turned around, he was gone."

"All they said was that this man told them to name their baby Joseph after the Joseph in the Bible. That was a shock to the couple because they had no idea she was with child."

"I sleepily wandered into the only, all night diner where I sat down at the counter and ordered a cup of coffee. The diner was empty except for the waitress and me. She asked me where the bearded man went. I said, "There was no such man in the diner when I entered."

"Wait a minute," she said. "I talked with him for over three hours. He said he was waiting for a bus." I quickly let her know that my bus was the last of the night. The next bus won't leave until 7 A.M."

"Then I began to inquire as to his dress and overall looks. She described the man to me and her description was exactly the same as the bearded man on my bus…even his eyes were the same color."

""How could the same man be talking to this young waitress and me at the same time? I was determined to solve this mystery…so I asked the waitress what they talked about. Here's what she said. "It's none of your business." Then she refreshed my coffee.""

"I couldn't let it drop there, with her abrupt response, so I told her about the bearded man that rode my bus for six hundred miles and the hour we talked to each other directly. After listening to me, she opened up and told me that her bearded man encouraged her to go back to her husband and that God would heal their marriage. She was puzzled as to how this mysterious stranger could know things about her."

Jim, "What happened then"

The bus driver continued, "then a truck driver came into the all night diner looking for some food and rest from the road. He sat next to me and we struck up a conversation. He told me about a hitchhiker that he picked up a few miles back. Don't you know?

It was the same bearded man that talked to the waitress and rode my bus. At lest we thought it was."

"The truck driver said the guy was nice. He spoke in a quiet sort of voice that kept him from falling asleep at the wheel. He said his bearded man wanted to wait in the truck while he came in for some coffee and a bite to eat."

"When I heard that he was still in the truck, the waitress and I ran outside to see if he was the same bearded man that we encountered but he was gone…no where to be found."

"We went back inside and talked to the truck driver at length. Everything he said about his bearded man fit our bearded man to a tee. The truck driver said that if it weren't for his rider, he would have crashed because he had been driving for hours and was really tired but didn't want to stop on an isolated road in the middle of the night."

"There we all were huddled together in an all night diner talking about a mysterious stranger with a bearded face. A waitress, a truck driver, a young married couple and a bus driver, strangers in the night with one thing in common, a mysterious bearded man."

"Suddenly, we could see the sunrise peeking through the morning haze and could hear the chirping of little birds as the long night turned into another day. There was a nip in the air and storm clouds off in a distance."

"We spent the entire night from the time I pulled into the bus station until the sun rose up to say hello talking about the stranger and how he had helped all of us in some small or big way."

"Some of us concluded that the stranger was a ghost in our imagination, born out of a lack of sleep and loneliness."

"Others said the stranger was an angel sent from God to help us in our time of need. I guess we will never really know who the stranger was and how he appeared in all our lives at the same time. All we could say is that our hearts burned inside."

"It was as if we knew him but couldn't recall his name. We'd seen him somewhere before but where we could not remember."

""It's been many years since we were all together in the "All Night" diner.""

"The waitress went home to her husband and became a fine mother to three kids."

"The truck driver went on to own his own business and stopped pushing himself to the point of exhaustion."

"The young married couple did in fact name their 1st child Joseph after the Biblical character. We all wondered how he knew that the child would be a boy before the mother became pregnant."

"Then there was me. I drove that bus for another 15 years and finally retired to Florida. We now have two grandkids."

"I believe that the "Mysterious Stranger" was not mysterious at all. I think he was a messenger from God. I could feel the love of God flowing from him as he spoke. I could see compassion in his eyes. It had to be a divine intervention."

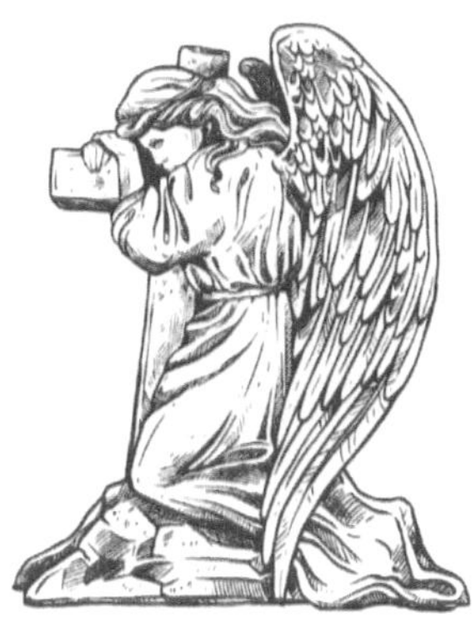

"All of our lives were dramatically changed from the encounter with the "Mysterious Stranger". You never know who will enter your life and what will happen as a result of a chance meeting. I guess it's good to be hospitable to strangers for they just may be ministering angels from heaven." **Hebrews 13:2**

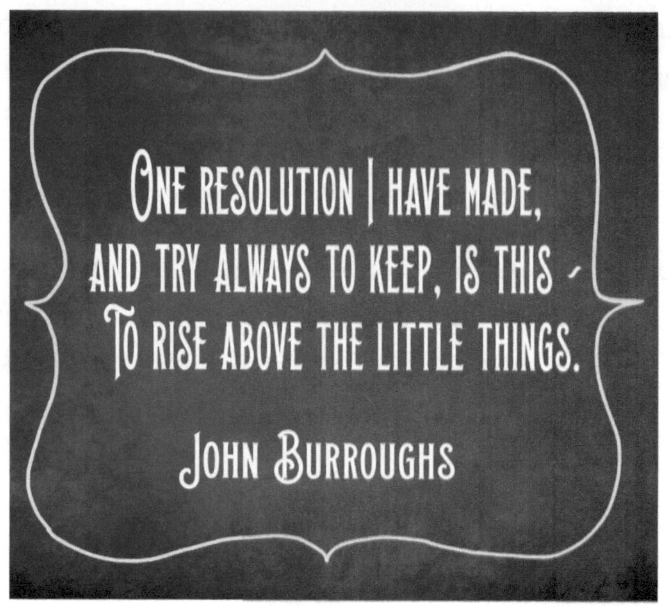

One resolution I have made,
and try always to keep, is this -
To rise above the little things.

John Burroughs

CHAPTER SEVEN

OUT OF NOWHERE

Jim moved on to his next appointment. He met with Ernie, the son of the bus driver. Ernie was open to share his encounter, He said,

"The year was 1952. It was a gray day with rain in the forecast. My old car needed breaks but I couldn't afford to fix what was wrong. I was late for my after school job and in a real hurry so, like most law-abiding citizens, I picked up speed and exceeded the legal limit."

"Wouldn't you know that the long arm of the law reached out to me with red lights flashing and his siren sounding?"

"I knew I could not get away but I was at an intersection facing a green light turning red. So I sped up faster to get through the light hoping the police officer would stop for the light."

"Suddenly, another vehicle turned right in front of me. He came out of nowhere and was in no hurry. I hit the breaks but couldn't stop. Instead I slid through the intersection burning rubber all the way."

"I was the son of a bus driver that was always careful and always kept the speed limit. I knew I was wrong but it was just too late. I was about to slam into the side of a brand new Cadillac with little children inside. They were sitting on the side of the immanent impact."

"I was out of control, sliding recklessly toward a terrible future. All I could do is cry out to God in hopes that He would help in some way so the children in the car would not get hurt. It wasn't much of a prayer. It was more of a desperate attempt to avoid the consequences of my actions."

"I couldn't help but think, "Why would God take the time to help me?" My dilemma was a portrait of my life. I was also out of control and running to avoid life's many challenges."

"I felt that the world would be a better place if I weren't around. My friends were all on drugs. My 16th birthday had just passed me by without even a Hello!"

""There was no reason to strive for excellence like my dad always told me. He tried real hard but look at him. He was just a bus driver. I kept feeling, *"Is That All There Is?"* There had to be more but more of what?""

"I closed my eyes and waited for the crash but I seemed to be stuck in the moment. I opened my eyes again to see my car sliding in slow motion and slowing down to almost a dead stop."

"At the same time, I saw a shadow of a man standing just outside my window. He had his hand on my car. I could also see the Cadillac racing at full speed in front of me as I slowly slid through the intersection."

"Now the policeman stopped at the light, waited for it to turn green and continued to come after me. I finally came to my senses and pulled into a shopping center parking lot and stopped."

"Yes, I was given *"The Idiot of The Day"* award and received a reckless driving ticket. The police officer also gave me a long lecture on the law. He scolded me and fussed at me and swore on his badge if he ever caught me speeding again, he would throw me under the jail, never mind in it."

"Then he said something strange. He asked me if I saw that man in the middle of the intersection. He said that it looked like he was holding my car back while the Cadillac passed. He actually saw what I saw in that slow motion moment."

"We both new that there was no way I could have missed hitting the Cadillac. Nevertheless, I missed it and avoided an accident."

"I told the officer that I also saw the man but when I looked again, he was gone. The officer said it was probably just a guy crossing the street at the wrong time."

"I knew better. It was God answering my halfhearted prayer. I couldn't help but wonder if the man in the intersection was the, "Mysterious Stranger" that my dad met so many years ago.

My dad went to court with me to face the consequences of my actions. The judge was amazed that a parent would show up in support of his teen. He told my dad that most of the kids in trouble come alone and have a bad attitude. They do not want their parents to know what they have done.

The judge reduced the charges to speeding and gave me a suspended sentence. That meant I didn't have to pay anything but if I ever showed up in his court again he would throw the book at me. I wasn't quite sure what that meant but I was glad to be going home.

My dad told the judge that he did not approve of my actions and had taken my driving privileges away except to go to school and work after school. He meant it too. I was grounded for two months."

"Later that night I talked to my mom about God. It was quiet in the house. My sister was at a sleep over with a girl friend and dad was on a bus run. She wanted to know all about what happened and particularly about the man in the intersection."

"Mom and I talked about everything except sex. We were close and she was not judgmental. She always offered some sort of counsel.

I told her all about the "Mystery Man" and she was amazed. She said that it had to be the hand of God protecting me. Well that opened the door for me to express my feelings. I told her how I felt all alone and useless.

I had no vision of a future or reason to go on. Yet the encounter with the man in the intersection made me think. Why would God save me from certain death or at least serious injury? He must want something from me or have something for me that I haven't seen as yet.

My mom told me about her feelings as a teen. She said that she too felt empty and useless. She would often think that there was no point to living until she gave her life and heart to Jesus.

Now I knew some of the religious kids at school and I didn't want to be like them. They were always trying to live by a set of rules and regulations that, in their own eyes, made them superior to others around them."

"We called these kids, "The Holier-Than-Thou Gang." Life was too hard to be a "Thou Shalt Not" disciple. But my mom said that she was not a, "Thou Shalt Not" type of person. Instead, she relied on what Jesus did and believed in Him as God's only Son. She found happiness and the will to live through God's grace or unmerited favor.

So life began to make sense to me. I could be myself and know that God still loved me. I liked what I heard.

So I went on with my life. I started going to church and became a member of the youth group. I began to read the Bible and it was there that I met Jesus. I learned of Him and I made Him Lord of my life. I was now His disciple, walking not by laws but by grace.

I still wonder if the man in the intersection was the, "Mysterious Stranger" my dad met many years ago. Maybe He was sent by God to help me in my time of need.

"The angel of the LORD encamps round about them that fear him, and deliver them." **Psalm 34:7**

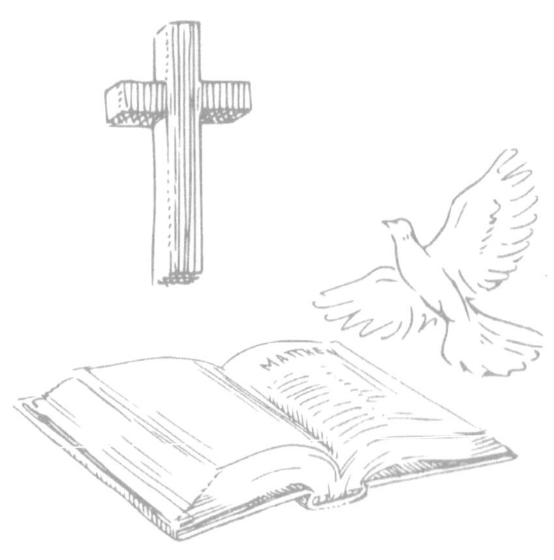

CHAPTER EIGHT

TEA FOR TWO

So Jim movers on to the next name on his interview list.

"Hello, Mrs. Anderson? This is Jim Smith, a reporter with the Christian Gazette. You and Bill are on my interview list concerning an article on a Mysterious Stranger. I spoke with your husband Bill before you guys went on vacation to Florida."

"Could I drop by and interview you for our paper? There's a lot of interest in the supernatural these days and our readers would find your story interesting."

Mrs. Anderson, in a soft voice, replied, "Please come over. I'll put on pot a of tea."

So Jim and Sarah sat down on a Sunday afternoon to talk about angels. It was then that he realized that she and her husband Bill were the subjects of a book based on a true love story during WWII.

They talked about how Bill was presumed killed in action

but showed up 10 years later and how a 1700's golden coin brought them back together. The Mystery of The Golden Coin was published to tell their story.

However, the purpose of their "Tea For Two" visit was not their story but hers, when she mysteriously contracted cancer. After all the loss and suffering she went through with Bill, cancer showing up in her body in its final stage was devastating. She just kept getting worse and medical assistance was of no avail.

Jim's interview was not specifically about Sarah's cancer but about the faith that got her through it. Jim had questions like, what was it about her faith that made the difference? How can faith do anything? What power does faith have to heal? He was hopping that Sarah could shed some light on the subject.

As they talked, Sarah began to cry. She had no clinical answers. She could not tell Jim the magic ingredient that saved her from certain death.

Jim needed answers and she didn't have any. All she had was a simple belief in God and a promise from the scriptures. She had no special formula, no hidden meditational cure and no secret chant. All she had was a God that no one can see and a Bible scripture that most folks never read.

Jim said to Sarah, "You mean that you were healed from cancer in its final stage by your faith in God?"

She quickly replied, "Yes, that is exactly right" Then she went on to explain.

"The Bible says that faith is not just a feeling but it is rather a substance. It has shape and forms those things that we hope for. In my case, my faith became the substance of what I desired which was complete healing."

"Wait, there's more," she said. "Faith was not only the substance of my hope but it was also the evidence of those things that I could not yet see. That means I can rest from all my worry, knowing that my faith will bring forth what I do not see with my eyes, which is life where death is now. You can read it for yourself in Hebrews 11:1."

"This Bible scripture was just one that was given to me. The man that gave it also shared several others and told me that they were hooks to hang my faith on." I never realized before that there was power in the written word of God.

Jim responds, "Power, explain…I don't understand."

Sarah began to explain by first saying, "I am not a Theologian, just a housewife. I do not claim to have all the answers nor do I try to assert my way of life on everyone else. I do know that a mysterious stranger came into my hospital room and gave me hope when there was no hope.

He showed me the precious promises of my Heavenly Father that are given to all who believe. He challenged me to embrace the scriptures, live by them and watch the hand of God move mountains."

So Sarah climbed aboard the glory train, giving the conductor her ticket of faith. She had a lot of trusting to do and a lot of believing but she made it through, with the power of God and a strong will to live and serve the Lord in this life.

Jim asked Sarah, "Who was this mysterious man?" but she didn't know. She just said that a man came into her hospital room in the middle of the night and called her by name.

According to Sarah, he said in a loud voice, "Sit up Sarah, Your faith has made you whole."

Sarah said that she thought the mystery man was an angel because she looked away for a split second and then back again only to find him gone. Now that would be almost impossible because he was too far from the door to have just walked out un-noticed.

She did remember that he said to her, "If you can only believe, you will live and not die" All she knew was that he was there in the middle of her room at the end of her bed and then he wasn't.

According to Sarah, the very next day her levels began to rise and her health slowly improved. It took a while but she did recover completely.

Jim's curiosity got the best of him. He wanted to know the other scriptures that the "Mystery Man" told her.

Sarah said she would be glad to share one more. It was her favorite scripture in the entire Bible. It was the hook that she hung her faith on during WWII.

"And we know that all things work together for good to them that love God, to them who are the called according to his purpose." **Romans 8:28**

She kept telling herself and everybody else that even though this cancer was a terrible thing, God is working it together for her good because she loved Him and was called according to His purposes.

Jim jumped in with another question, "So it was God that gave you cancer so He could heal you from it. Is that what you are saying? Sounds like God wanted you to suffer, doesn't it?"

Sarah replied, "No silly, God is a loving God. He does not punish His children with sickness or disease. There are many causes… could be a weak immune system, poor diet, reckless lifestyle, drugs, almost anything, even demonic attacks. But it is never from God."

"However, God, because He loves us, gets down and dirty with us in the situation to comfort us, guides us and sometimes even heal us. He says in His Word that He will never leave us or forsake us."

It didn't matter to Sarah if she lived or died. She believed that God knew best. Her life and times were in His hands to do whatsoever He so desired. However, she had the angel's challenge to believe and be healed so she figured that God wanted her to live. So she believed and lived and is here today with her husband that was declared dead in the war but lived to tell about it.

Sometimes it is better to see with the eyes of Faith than with the eyes of our understanding. I guess that is because our understanding is finite or limited to our own experiences.

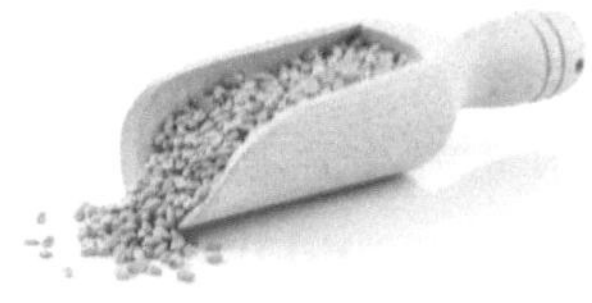

Faith on the other hand, has no boundaries and is not proportionate to that which stands in our way. Jesus said it this way,

> *" I say to you, if you have faith as a mustard seed, you will say to this mountain, 'Move from here to there,' and it will move; and nothing will be impossible for you. "* **Matthew 17:20**

The mustard seed is very small and the mountain is very large. The difference is that the faith of a mustard seed has the power of God in it and the ability to grow and multiply into an endless source of strength.

"So here I am," said Jim, the great Jim Smith, a newspaper reporter following a "Mysterious Stranger" who helps people in need. The only problem is, they can't absolutely say their helper was an angel.

The gospel of Jesus Christ is the good news that God provided the way for man to be freed from the penalty of sin (John 14:6; Romans 6:23)

Chapter Nine

Danger And The Stranger

Jim looked over the list of interviews he had already done. First it was a young woman who was walking to her car at night after a fun-shopping spree when two men attack her. Their attack was spoiled and they were arrested. The two attackers later admitted that they broke off their attack and ran when two big men suddenly came to her rescue. The young woman saw no men at her side.

A little boy and mother are prevented from getting on a bus by a strange intense-looking man in white clothes who said, "Don't get on this bus" The bus doors close, and it pulls out into traffic and was immediately hit by a tractor trailer, killing everyone on board. But no one else saw the man in white and he was nowhere to be found.

Jim was looking for something he could hang his hat on; a common thread; a single something that would help him in his quest to interview the mysterious stranger. After a thorough review, Jim finally moves on to his next interview, Bill Anderson, the D-Day hero. Here's how that interview went.

So Bill, said Jim, "tell us about your heroic deeds during the big war."

Bill replies, "There isn't much to say and I am not really a war hero."

Jim, "Didn't you shield a squad of men from a mortar attack? You're a survivor of the Normandy Invasion. You were also a Navy Seal, right?"

Bill, "No I was an Army Ranger, Special Forces. You must be thinking of someone else that was a Seal. My son was in the navy and was awarded the Silver Star after saving several of his shipmates when their ship collided with another."

Jim, "So let's talk about you first. How did you ever survive that mortar attack?"

Bill, "I didn't. All I remember is hearing a blast. I was standing right in the spot where the mortar landed. It should have blown me to bits."

Jim, "But it didn't, why?"

Bill, "I think it was because of the prayers of my wife and our church. When the explosion began, I saw a "Mysterious Stranger" dressed in all white. He grabbed me and pulled me toward him. He took the brunt of the explosion. I was severely injured but pretty much in one piece."

Jim, "So it was an angel that saved you that day, right?"

Bill, "Yes and No because the blast blew away most of my face, my hands were badly burned and I lost my memory."

"The mystery man saved my life but the army doctors had no idea whose life it was and I couldn't tell them because of the trauma I suffered in the blast. Even my fingerprints were gone. My clothing was shredded. My military ID and dog tags were gone. Nobody knew who I really was, not even me."

Jim, "What can you tell me about the Mysterious Stranger?"

Bill, "Not much to tell. He was about my height and general build. He was very strong because he pulled me away in a split second before the first mortar exploded. He had to have had supernatural strength to do what he did."

"I believe that I was saved because of the many and continual prayers of my family and friends back home. They offered up prayer before the throne of God every night and some two or three times a day."

Jim, "What happened then?"

Bill, "The Mysterious Stranger tossed me through the air in the direction of several other rangers that did not get hit. One was a field medic on his way to the triage."

"This medic carried me on his back for three and a half miles. He thought I was dead when he laid me on the operating table because I was hardly breathing, had lost a lot of blood and was not moving."

Jim, "What happened to this man in white, the mystery man?"

Bill, "He was all around the area, I was in and out of consciousness and every time I'd wake up, he would be there helping a ranger to go on or a medic to stay focused. He even dropped in on me several times to be sure I was ok. He was the real hero of WWII, not me."

Jim, "Yea, but I can't interview him."

Bill, "I think he was sent by God to help our men in battle. I can even remember seeing him on the beach when sniper bullets were zinging by. Those guys had scopes on their rifles and we are dead center in their sites. There was no way they could have missed; yet they did. It just shows me how the hand of God was there to keep us alive."

Jim, "What about all the men that died that day? Did they not get an angel from God?"

Bill, "No, I think there were many angels but many on both sides of the war still died. I believe this was because war was not God's plan for man. He didn't cause it to happen and to protect man's free will to choose, He had to let it play out."

"As tragic as it was, men had to die as a result of many nations' choices. However, God still has a plan for man and knows the future. He listens to His children when they cry out to Him and He respects the many prayers of a community that reverences Him."

"Who lives and who dies is in God's hands. We may never know why I lived and my fellow rangers did not. That is another mystery to be revealed in His timing."

Jim asked Bill a direct question," Would you say that you were definitely visited by an angelic being from heaven?"

Bill answered, "No I can not say definitely that the mysterious stranger was an angel. However, if I go by what I read in the Bible, it sure looks like my stranger was indeed an angelic being."

"There are many Biblical examples of angelic encounters. They are often used as proof text, that God can and does use angels to accomplish His will. What we don't know is why some folks see angels and others do not."

"It is quite possible that many people today have entertained an angel without realizing it. The most referred to scripture concerning angels walking among us is Hebrews 13:2"

> *"Be not forgetful to entertain strangers: for thereby some have entertained angels unawares."*

Bill continues, "It is obvious that angels are in our midst. One of their duties is to help us get through tough times. All the more reason we should be nice to strangers and seek to be a blessing. One day, a messenger may visit us."

Jim figured that his article was finished and ready for his editor's eyes. He decided to deliver his story in person instead of by eMail but wanted to stop in a local hangout where other columnists frequented. Little did he know that he was about to have his own encounter with the Mysterious Stranger.

CHAPTER TEN

THE EDITOR AND THE TERRORIST

The next day Jim was talking to his editor. He summarized his report and submitted the typed copy and said, "Well, that is my report."

Jim's editor replied saying, "It will run in tomorrow's paper."

Then Jim began to tell his editor about the night before when he stopped in to visit with some other reporters. "What I didn't say in my article was my personal encounter with what I believe was the mysterious stranger that I had chased around three states interviewing people that had an encounter with an angel. I couldn't bring myself to admit what happened to me was real."

"You see I was a doubting Thomas type of Christian. God was just not active in my world. At least I thought that way until I listened to all these fine folks and actually read the Biblical references. But it was my own experience that opened my eyes to the possibility of a personal God who loved me."

"After finishing my article, I stopped in at a local restaurant where newspaper reporters hang out. I was on my way here to talk to you when I met a mysterious stranger. He was seated at the counter."

Editor, "Really, you actually met him?"

Jim replies, "I said, "Mysterious" because his clothing was old fashioned. It looked like he just stepped out of the 18th century. He even had a pocket watch that was an antique."

"Well he kept looking at his watch and then at me. He seemed like he was in a hurry but didn't leave. I couldn't stand the suspense so I went over to him and sat down next to him.

The stranger immediately said, "You're late." I said in response, "For what?"

The stranger said, "Stick with me. Things are about to get rough." Suddenly the doors opened to the restaurant and three men ran in shooting pistols at anyone in their way. They were yelling something in a foreign language.

The stranger and I were at the very end of the counter so it took a few minutes to get to us. All of a sudden I was face to face with a terrorists who was bent on killing everyone.

I screamed, "Please don't shoot me." It was then that this "Mysterious Stranger" stepped in front of me and took the brunt of their attack. They emptied two magazines of ammo into him, one bullet after another.

They kept shooting because the stranger didn't fall. He just stood there in front of me with a big smile on his face. The bullets just bounced off of him.

The police were on the scene really fast but not fast enough. Eight people were killed and four seriously wounded. They shot and killed the three terrorists in a gun battle, all the time with me at the end of the counter behind the mysterious stranger.

When it was all over, one of the police officers asked me how it was that I did not get hit. I said, "It was because of him" and pointed in the direction of the mystery man but he was no longer there."

The officer said, "There was no one else but me at the restaurant." All of the first responders swore that I was alone from the time they entered the restaurant.

The "Mysterious Stranger" just vanished into thin air. I know he was there and I could see the bullets hitting his chest. It was then that I knew that God was real and that He loved me. I got to tell yah, it changed my life. I am now a God-Seeker.

Chapter Eleven

The Niece and The 14 Year Old

Jim hardly had time to calm down from the terrorist's attack when he received word that his niece was rushed to the emergency room. She had a ruptured appendix. They took her in right away and off she went into surgery. It was really bad, the worst her doctors had ever seen.

She spent six hours in the operating room and three in recovery before they admitted her to a room on the 4th floor. All the rooms on the general surgery floor were taken so they added her to the baby delivery floor.

When she woke up she heard screaming and yelling as babies were being born. The thing was, she didn't know they were birth pains. She thought the doctors were not using any drugs before doing surgery. She freaked out and they had to sedate her.

She was in and out of consciousness for most of the time.

She fell asleep for a while until she heard a man enter her hospital room. It was the middle of the night.

She was still a bit groggy from the surgery and drugs. He sat in the only chair in the room. He was quite at first but then began to read from the Bible out loud. She struggled to listen wondering what he was reading.

All of a sudden her hearing cleared up and she could understand what he was reading. It was the King James Bible. He read this passage. I know it was this one because I spent three days trying to find it. It said:

> *"But he was wounded for our transgressions, he was bruised for our iniquities: the chastisement of our peace was upon him; and with his stripes we are healed."* **Isaiah 53:6**

He just kept reading that one verse over and over again. When He saw that my niece was now awake he stopped reading but did not look up. He simply said,

"I was sent here to make sure you'd be alright. You are going to be fine. Now you should get some rest. Go back to sleep"

Then he began to read again and Jim's niece drifted off to sleep.

The next morning, she told the doctor about her mystery man. He checked the schedule for that night and found no record of any visits. She even asked all of the nurses and no one knew of him.

I think that an angel visited her. Whoever he was, he gave her a lot of hope and she was comforted. He assured her that she would be okay. Oddly enough, she looked at the clock next to her bed and saw the time. It was 3:17 A. M., the exact time of her birth as recorded on her birth certificate.

She told her doctor, " Can't wait to tell my uncle. He is a reporter and just did a story about visiting angels. He told us a story about a "Mysterious Stranger" that rode a bus one night and talked to him and talked to folks in an all night diner. He'll probably say that my mystery man was their Mysterious Stranger.

She told Jim later that she was glad that God sent an angel to let her know that she would live and not die. She never thought that she would see daylight again. But here she is, by the grace of God.

She then explained that it was not the first time that she met an angel. She said, "When I was young, a little kid, I always said a prayer. It was the same one every night." It went something like this:

> *"Now I lay me down to sleep, I pray the Lord my soul to keep, watch over me Jesus through the night and keep me safe till morning's light." (Author Unknown)*

"I soon fell asleep with a feeling of security. I knew that I'd be safe. All my childhood fears, like the Boogieman, would just go away."

"As I grew up, the childhood prayer faded away. I became an adult and adults are not supposed to be fearful. They are supposed to be strong and aware of what is real and what is not."

"However, this wasn't the case with me. I was afraid of most everything. I'd watch the local evening news on TV with all its evil reports and cry because I thought the evil would come to my door next."

"I hated to come home at night because it was dark and I couldn't see who or what lurked in the shadows. If I went out at night, I had to be with someone, not just anyone, but someone I felt could protect me."

"I thought that I was a Christian and even went to church faithfully. However, I didn't really apply what the pastor preached. I never read my Bible. It was a decoration on my coffee table. My religion didn't serve any real purpose."

"One day I decided to have a private counseling session with my pastor. As I shared with him my fears he immediately knew what was wrong and told me in no uncertain terms. He said that fear did not come from God. It was a result of our own worry or worse a demonic attacks."

"He wanted to know when I was saved and what happened. I told him I joined the church and said, wasn't that enough?"

"It was then that he and I both realized that I was not really saved. We prayed together and I accepted Jesus into my heart as my savor. But the fear did not go away. It actually got worse."

"I cried a lot and prayed a lot. One night I cried myself to sleep. When I woke up, out of nowhere, I saw a beautiful bright light filling up my room. I looked at my clock and saw that it was 4 A.M."

"Suddenly, from within the light came a man all dressed in white linen. He turned back towards the light and said, sing with me. I could hear several voices but saw no one else but the man in white."

"Then I started to remember the words to the song and heard, as it were a choir, singing my childhood prayer."

> *"Now I lay me down to sleep, I pray the Lord my soul to keep, watch over me Jesus through the night and keep me safe till morning's light."*

"The mystery man actually sang my prayer to me over and over again. Then I heard a bellowing voice from within the light." It said:

> *"Fear not; for I am with you: be not dismayed; for I am your God: I will strengthen you; yes, I will help you; yes, I will uphold you with the right hand of my righteousness."*

"I knew that he spoke the words of the scriptures. I wrote them down and looked for the scripture later and found it in **Isaiah 41:10**."

Then the encounter ended. The light faded away, the man in white linen disappeared and I fell back to sleep.

The next day, I called my pastor. After listening to me he asked me one question, *"How do you feel"* I answered, loved and safe. I do not feel that horrible fear that gripped my soul for so many years.

I feel like a new person, happy and alive. I wondered if my angelic encounter could have something to do with my uncle Jim and all the others he interviewed for his article.

I guess it really doesn't matter. What does matter is God loves me, my fear is gone and I have been strengthen from within so I can live free from evil forces to walk with Jesus.

My childhood prayer was made into a song and is now being sung in children's churches around the world. It is wonderful to know that God is on your side and that He really does have your best interest at heart.

Jim ends his niece's story and asked his editor another question, "Did I tell you about Joseph?

Remember the young married couple that met the Mysterious Stranger? Joseph is their son. Well it's really weird what happened to him when he was fourteen. I talked to the bus driver a few weeks ago and he told me the story.

Joseph was a good son to his parents. I say, "Was" because he, like many teenagers of the day, went his own way and did his own thing. Joseph was no different than the kids of his day. He wanted to rebel and he did.

His mother was a Christian and prayed for him daily. His dad always worked and wasn't around much. Joseph was left to fend for himself most of the time.

Well, fending for self put Joseph in a lot of trouble. He started to hang with the wrong crowd and was just about to start taking and selling drugs.

Joseph became unruly and standoffish. He pushed the limits of his mother's love and drove her to the throne of God. She cried before the Lord asking God to intervene in Joseph's life before it was too late. She knew that her son was on the verge of being lost forever to a life sentence of drugs, crime, immorality and sorrow. She asked God to show her son what that sort of life really is all about.

A few days later Joseph was fast asleep at home in his own bed until a Mysterious Stranger came to visit. It was in the middle of the night when the stranger spoke to Joseph and said, "See what is on the road you have chosen in life."

Joseph, even though asleep, sat up to see what the stranger spoke of. He began to weep when he saw another teen falling down in an alley and the emergency medics declaring her dead from an overdose. She was his age.

Then he saw homeless children sleeping in the streets, their parents high on drugs and unable to hold down a steady job.

Then he saw himself in a crack house with other dealers shooting up and selling to users who had to have a fix just to feel alive again.

Then he saw himself looking into a mirror at himself and crying because his life was empty and useless. He was just like all the others, dead inside and alone.

The mystery man spoke again and said, "This is the end of the road that you have chosen." Then he saw a coffin with his name on it and a funeral with no one in attendance.

Suddenly, he saw demons laughing at him as he fell through space and time into a fiery hell. He saw himself screaming and pleading with God for another chance.

Joseph was terrified and broke into a cold sweat. He realized that it was just a dream but also a vision of what was to come if he continued to pursue a life of drugs and rebellion.

The angelic visitor vanished and Joseph fell into a deep sleep.

The next morning He opened his mother's Bible and the page fell to John 3:16.

> "For God so loved the world, that he gave his only begotten Son, that whosoever believeth in him should not perish, but have everlasting life."

Joseph began to realize that he was not a, "Whosoever"

so he decided to become one. His mother's prayers were answered.

Joseph is now in Bible College studying to be a minister of the gospel. His testimony and growing knowledge of the scriptures are leading him to share Christ with others.

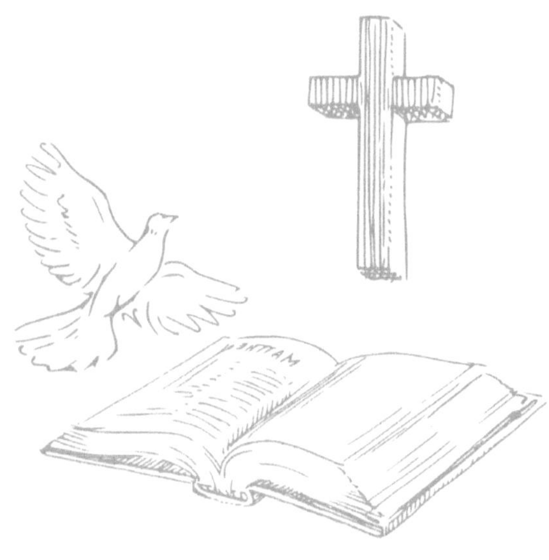

Chapter Twelve

A Second Encounter

After submitting my article, I received a call from the truck driver that I had interviewed before. It was concerning a second encounter with the same stranger. Here's what he said.

"Driving a tractor-trailer rig is not easy. It takes a lot of skill especially when driving on icy roads, narrow bridges and in rainy weather.

If it weren't for a Mysterious Stranger I wouldn't be here today. He was a hitchhiker that I picked up one night. He was talkative and kept me alert and awake. I was pushing to finish my overland run and surely would have fallen asleep if it weren't for him.

That was many years ago. Now I have my own trucking company and employ seven drivers. I am successful and happy. However, things are not going so good.

My wife is about to disown me. Even my dog hates me.

Every time I come home he growls at me as though I were an intruder.

I went for the big bucks and the trucking industry has a lot of that. I just kept getting richer and richer but my heart was falling into despair because my entire life was trucking. I lived and breathed business. My slogan was, "On The Road Again." It came from a popular country song.

I often wished that I could talk to that Mysterious Stranger again. His perspective on life was so clear. He just made sense when he talked. Maybe he could tell me where I went wrong and how to fix it.

I didn't want to lose my wife and have my dog hate me forever. I had to fix it, but how? I wasn't a religious man and didn't pray a lot. But one night I did pray and asked God to help me.

A few weeks went by and I had to fill in for a sick driver. I took the overland run that put me out of town for three days. It was an easy run but somewhat boring. I offered to take my wife with me but she didn't like being on the road with all the drunks and drugs.

She argued with me and begged me not to go. She had a bad feeling about me going. When women have bad feeling, you better pay attention to them because it's usually a sign from heaven. Well I ignored her feelings, fluffing them off as nonsense.

Now I wish I had listened and heeded her plea. She was

right. One hundred miles out I stopped at a rest stop to get some gas and snacks. It was late afternoon and the sun was setting. Two men stepped in front of me by my truck and demanded money. One of the men had a gun in his left hand.

I told them no and to get away from my truck. I told them that I work hard for what I have and I am not about to give it away to two hoodlums. They didn't know that I was carrying a gun in my shirt, concealed from sight.

The hoodlum with the gun started to pull his gun and at the same time I pulled mine. I beat him to the draw but he still had me in his sights.

There we were at a standoff with guns aimed at each other. What to do? Was his pistol racked and ready to fire? Or was he just bluffing. My Glock was racked and I was ready to fire. He hesitated so I did to. That caused the standoff. My previous training was to shoot first and ask questions later.

Then he started waving his weapon around trying to intimidate me all the while cursing me and demanding money. I could see that he was building up courage to fire his gun so I blasted him with two shots to his mid section and then I turned to the other hoodlum and aimed my gun at his head. He fell down to the floor and surrendered.

As the first hoodlum fell he squeezed off two shots that hit the ground. That showed me that he was loaded and ready. It was just a matter of time before he would have shot me.

The police came and the ambulance. The one who I shot would live and see another day but this time from a prison cell. I was a wreck inside. It was the first time I actually shot someone. It was very traumatic to see blood and know you were the cause of it.

I couldn't sleep at all that night. I tossed and turned in my truck. I felt sorry for shooting my gun at another human being but relieved that it was him and not me that has to recover from bullet wounds.

My emotions were all over the place but I had to move on and finish my run. My mind raced back and forth through the events that happened as I trucked on down the road.

Then a hitchhiker came into view and I sure could use the company so I came to a screeching halt. Low and behold, it was the same Mysterious Stranger that I picked up so many years ago. He jumped in and we were back on the road.

I said, "Boy am I glad to see you" He replied, "Oh" and we began to talk. I unloaded on him all the events that happened and said, "What would you have done?" He didn't answer me. He just sat there and watched the road go by as we barreled down the highway.

I tried to be calm but was fighting back my anger. Finally I said, "Are you an angel?" He replied, "I am just a guy looking for a lift."

"No you are not," I said. "You are the same Mysterious Stranger that I met many years ago."

He then said, "Yes, I am a messenger of God and I have a message for you. Here's what God wants you to know. He told His Apostle, Paul over 2,000 years ago so you would know for sure that this message is from Him.

> *"For we wrestle not against flesh and blood, but against principalities, against powers, against the rulers of the darkness of this world, against, spiritual wickedness in high places."* **Ephesians 6:12**

These evil forces work through evil people like the two men that attacked you."

Then the angel said, *"Look At This?* There is a real devil and he, with his demons, are going around seeking whom he may devour (1 Peter 5:8). He comes to steal, kill and destroy (John 10:10). Do not be afraid to stand against evil. God is with you when you fight back. His power has already defeated the devil and his gang of thieves. Take your peace and allow God to bless you."

Then my Mysterious Stranger told me to make this trip my last. He said that my wife was in need of me and I MUST go home.

I had to slow down due to traffic and I began shifting that big rig. Once I got it under control, I looked over at my hitchhiker but he was not there. He vanished out of sight.

I felt a lot better, was wide-awake and stopped all the worry. My Mysterious Stranger came to me with a message from God. He delivered it and went on his way.

That was the second time he saved my life. The first was keeping me awake so I wouldn't crash. The second was crashing my fears so I would not blame myself for protecting myself from would-be killers.

I took the Stranger's counsel as from God and decided to follow it. I went home to my wife, sold my business, house and property. Then we moved to Florida to a retirement community that had lots of activities. The hardest part was learning how to play again after working for so many years.

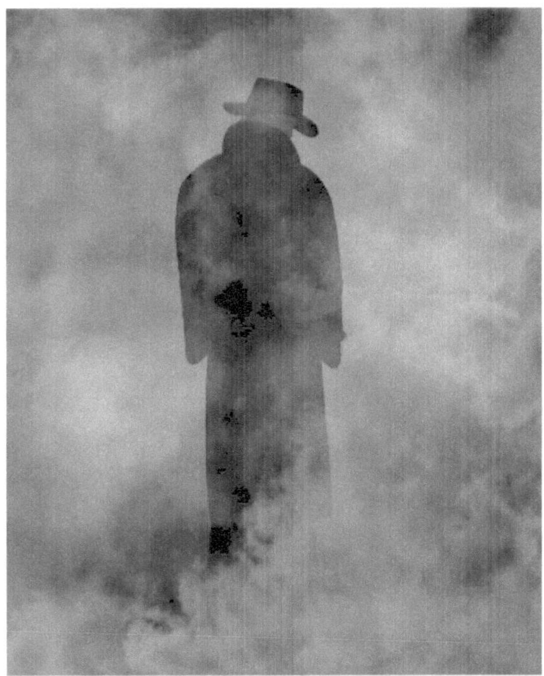

Chapter Thirteen

Off The Grid

Jim made a long distance phone call to Bill Jr. to inquire about his mysterious stranger. He was following a lead from Bill Jr.'s dad. Finally, after several attempts he got through to Bill Jr. and asked the big question. "Did you encounter an angelic visitation while in Vietnam?" He also wanted to know why he wanted to live off the grid.

Bill Jr. began to explain. He said, "I am sorry. I just could not take it anymore. The Vietnam War took it all away, my hopes, my dreams and even my will to live. My dad is the WWII combat hero, Bill Anderson. I am his son.

I grew up learning survival techniques from my dad. He was an expert shot and was trained in how to survive in any condition.

I was more at home off the grid than in the city. The outdoors was my kind of life. I was deep into camping, fishing and hunting. I would go on fly-ins with a buddy to the most remote areas of Montana, Canada and Alaska and spend weeks in God's beautiful nature. I was indeed a "Wilderness Man.

Well now you know pretty much all there is to know about me except for that time I got lost in the Alaskan Bush. There were two weeks that I was lost in the bush. They were more traumatic than being in combat in Nam and treading water for hours in the north China Sea when my ship collided with another.

It's really scary to be in unfamiliar territory and not know which way was the way home. I had always known before but this time I just couldn't figure it out.

I had two different encounters with brown bears and had to run for miles to escape a wild pig that attacked me. Wherever I was, it was a dangerous place.

After several days of searching for a way out of the bush, I realized that I might be here for a while. The only thing to do was to make a base camp and protect myself from the weather. It was the end of spring and fall was just about three miles away.

It took me a few days to get my base camp in order. Then came the snow and bitter cold. Nights dropped down in temperature to a minus 30 degrees. I was in big trouble.

This was supposed to be a two-week adventure in the Alaskan Bush. However, it has quickly turned into a life or death struggle.

It all started when I went down stream chasing after a deer

with my trusty bow and arrow. All my survival gear was in the cabin.

The deer ran into the bush and I followed, not aware that the bush was so thick that after a half-mile or so I could no longer hear the river or see through the trees. I tried to get back to the river but the more I wandered the further I went in the wrong direction.

All I had with me was a bow, six arrows and a field knife. The forest was dry and I could hear thunder off in a distance. That was not good as it sets up the possibility for a wild fire. Lightening strikes began to fall and actually blow up trees around me.

How I longed to be with my dad again in a safe environment. We use to sit around a campfire and sing songs and talk for hours about what to do if I were to ever get lost in the forest. All that knowledge would come in handy now.

So there I was in the middle of a lightening storm with bolts of electricity from the clouds splitting trees and hitting the ground all around me.

Suddenly a wild fire broke out and the wind blew it my way. I was engulfed in a firestorm. I couldn't run because there was nowhere to run without hitting a wall of flames. It was obvious that this was to be the place of my death."

Jim speaks up, "So what did you do?"

Bill Jr. "So I sat down and began to pray that God would take me quickly so I would not suffer long. I asked forgiveness for my many sins and prayed that He would receive me into His kingdom.

The fire closed in and it was hot. I could feel the hairs on my head starting to singe. I closed my eyes and waited for whatever was next.

Then, out of nowhere a man appeared. He came right out of the flames yet was not burned. He extended his hand to me and said, "Come with me and stay as close as you can." So I did just as he said. We went directly into the wall of flames that was about to consume me but the flames had no affect.

We walked slowly through the fire to safety. When it was all over, we were at the river's edge. The "Mysterious Stranger" pointed to the north and said, "Your cabin is that way, about two miles." I looked down the river and then back his way to say, "Thank You" but he was gone.

I was trembling inside but happy too. I came to the Alaskan Bush for an adventure and certainly got one. I couldn't wait to get back to civilization where I could call my dad and tell him what happened."

It was then that Bill Jr. made the decision to learn all he could and return to Alaska to live off the grid. He knew it would be a real challenge and that's what He was looking for.

Eventually, He made it back but not before finding a wife that was just as crazy as me. They now are Alaskan Wilderness Guides taking city folk on two-week adventures into the Alaska Bush.

Bill Jr. "This is the place of my dreams and where I will dwell with my family. Life is good and God's grace is even better."

Jim was amazed and said to himself, "Why didn't I get him in the article." His story was really amazing. He decided to write a sequel down the road and find more folks to interview. He even contemplated writing a book.

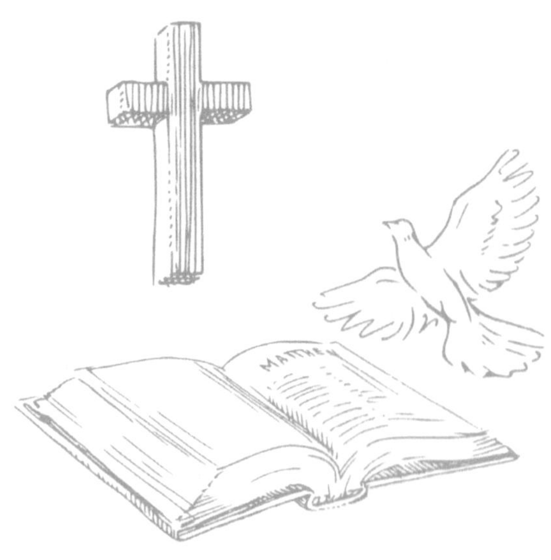

Chapter Fourteen

Grandpa's Diary

As Jim settled down from a long journey among the many supernatural events, he got a call from Bill and Sarah Anderson. They were cleaning out their attic. In the process of tossing out old stuff and digging through boxes, Bill came upon a leather bound key lock diary. The leather was old and parched and the lock was broken. Bill called to Sarah to come and see.

Sarah brushed off the dust and was amazed to find that the writing on the cover said, "This is the diary of Bill Anderson" There was also a date that went from 1861 to 1865. The penmanship inside the book was still clear and legible even though the pages were worn and fragile. So Bill and Sarah sat down to read what his great grandpa wrote. The entries were not by date or sequence. It still was like reading the script of a movie. Sarah began reading.

"My dear Susan. I decided to keep a brief record of the events that I am currently involved in here in the Virginia countryside. The inhabitants do not welcome our Northern army and rebels that hide in farmhand clothes constantly attack us.

We have the military advantage but the confederate army is still a formidable foe. I have given instructions to my superiors to get this diary to you in the event of my untimely death.

However, I do pray every day and some times more than once for God's protective grace and that this conflict would soon be over.

JULY, 1861... THE BATTLE OF MANASSAS

I fought along side some of the bravest men I have ever known. We charged the rebels and ended up fighting hand to hand in a violent struggle for life and victory. Many men fell on the battlefield from both sides.

Today I killed three rebels. One looked to be about 14 years old. I was deeply saddened that they died but it's war and folks die in wars. I hope that God will forgive me.

The Days After The Battle--I survived *Manassas* but was assigned to a burial detail with 25 other soldiers. We made sure those who died were honored in their sacrifice. I kept a record of names and personal belongings for my superior, Captain Clarke.

Them Johnny Rebs beat us good. But it ain't over yet. It's just one battle.

Now I spend much of my time in camp enduring long hours of boredom, followed by daily drills and guard duty. I thought this was going to be an adventure. Instead, it's a war of nerves as we all wait for the next conflict.

THE BATTLE OF SHILOH THE BATTLE OF PITTSBURG LANDING

God saved my life today. I was on the battlefield. It was dark with canons blasting everywhere. The sound came to charge so we did but the trumpet that sounded was not ours. It was those darn rebels that sounded the charge. So both armies charged at each other in the middle of the night. It was a confused mess.

I ran and ran and suddenly fell from a cannon blast. It should have blown my legs clean off but it didn't. I was shaken but untouched by the blast. I looked up towards the moonlight as if to say, "Thank You" to God but instead saw a mysterious stranger. He was smiling at me.

I started to get up and looked away to get my footing. When I looked back, he was gone. He was dressed in all white clothing and had a bearded face. I think God sent me an angel. I sure needed one.

Dear Diary…I guess I will live and not die in this forsaken place. My dream is to return to my wife and have kids and live a good life in these here United States."

Sarah concludes…"There are no more entries."

Bill…"Wow, he also saw the Mysterious Stranger. That guy gets around."

> *"Be not forgetful to entertain strangers: for thereby some have entertained angels unawares. "* **Hebrews 13:2**

"You never know when or where a "Mysterious Stranger" will drop into your world unannounced. The Bible says that these "Mysterious Strangers" are ministering spirits that are doing the will of God in the earth related to His children.

If angels are real, and I am sure they are, we should know more about them. However, they are not God. Nor are they to be worshiped."

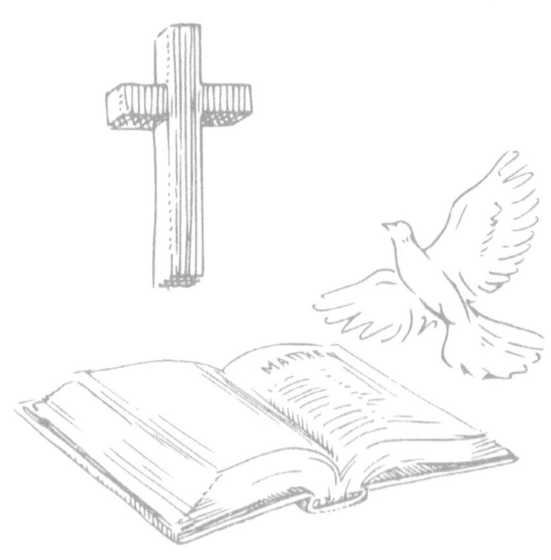

CHAPTER FIFTEEN
THE REST OF THE STORY

Bill Continues, "God's love is the only solution to filling the void in man's empty soul. Sadly, some reject God's love and never find it. Nevertheless, angels still come and go in the lives of those that believe.

Jim responds with a question. "How do we know that angels really interact with man? Couldn't it be that in times of stress, we imagine such things?" Bill said, Jim should read Hebrews 1:4

> *"Are not all angels ministering spirits sent to serve those who will inherit salvation?" Hebrews 1:14*

Bill continues, "So it was with Michael and Billie Jo. Both searched for something to fill the void. After years of searching, Michael did find God's love and it filled his very being.

However, the personal journey of Billie Jo led her away from God and Michael. She was caught up in the drug scene and fell into anxiety, fear and depression during her teen years.

Billie Jo was even visited more than once by your mysterious stranger and still rejected God and any kind of morality."

Bill makes a suggestion, "Mister Reporter Man, you should interview my friend, Michael. He has the rest of your story. Not everyone chooses life nor do all human experiences end in happiness."

So Jim heads out to find Bill's friend. He was just a phone call away.

Jim talks to himself as he departs, "What is it about this story? It just doesn't want to end."

MICHAEL'S TESTIMONY

Jim makes his call to Michael, "Hello sir, Bill Anderson suggested I speak with you concerning the possibility of an encounter with an angel. I am that reporter that is doing a story for a national Christian newspaper."

Michael responds with, "Ok, why don't you drop by. I am the 3rd house on the left when you turn off Quincy Ave onto Jones Street. It's a blue and white house."

So Jim and Michael meet and discuss Billie Jo. Michael decides to tell his story as it really happened, from his personal experiences with Billie Jo. He stands up in his living room and speaks as if he is talking to his entire church. He told Jim that he'd get the full affect that way.

"Hurry Melody." Said Michael. "Get the kids ready. I don't want to be late for Church. The pastor is counting on me to give my personal testimony." Then he speaks for Melody, his wife saying, OK! OK!, we will all be ready."

Michael continues, "and so the time came for me to stand before the congregation of Saints and give my personal testimony. There must have been more than three hundred folks looking straight at me. I was really nervous."

Michael stands behind an imaginary podium in his home to make it feel like it was happening now, even though it had already happened in his church three weeks ago.

"First of all, let me say that Melody and I have been to-gether for over fifteen years. We have two fine children, Bobby, age 12 and Larry, age 9. We have two dogs and four cats and may soon add a talking bird.

We've been active members of this community church for most of that time. Those of you that know us… know that we are a very happily married couple.

Well, life was not so wonderful for me before Melody came into my life. What I am about to say has been cleared with my family so there will be no surprises.

However, My personal testimony is intertwined with a woman from the past. Her name was Billie Jo. I will tell you her story as part of my testimony. It's the only way to show you how God worked in my life.

About 16-years ago, I was living alone, depressed and lost. I just couldn't figure out why things were the way that they were. My life was empty and I had a lot of issues.

One cold winter's day, I received an invitation in the mail. It was actually a notification of my high school reunion. It was from an old girlfriend from high school. Her name was Billie Jo. We didn't date that much but were really good friends.

The notification just said, let's go, what do you think? I hesitated to say yes because those things are so depressing. It's just one long trip down memory lane and this lane was filled with so many sorrows. I didn't want to relive that part of my past. After all, my life had changed since then. I was a different person now.

Back in those days Billie Jo was a suffering soul. She was caught up in one trap after another as she tried to live her life her way. The problem was, her way put her on a road that led to destruction.

Billie Jo was so independent and head strong that nobody could tell her what to do. She hardly took my advice. I had to argue with her over most everything just to get her to see that there were alternatives to what she was thinking.

All of my friends loved Billie Jo. She was alive and outgoing, a lot of fun. However, we all felt that Billie Jo was not the marrying kind. We didn't want a house of contention and miscommunication.

I was from the old school that looked at life and marriage as a partnership where friendship and love could flourish. Yes, we still believed that the man was chosen by God to be the head of the household.

However, being the head of the household, to me anyway, did not include spouse abuse, dictatorship, or an iron hand rule. I figured that God created woman because man was incomplete, being by himself. A "Help Mate" would be of great value.

But Billie Jo had her own thoughts on the subject and marched to the beat of a different drum. She was right in her own eyes all the time. There was no room for mistakes or other folk's suggestions. It was her way or the highway.

Billie Jo was a free spirit. Yes, she was liberal and openly hostile towards men who looked "Macho." She would challenge boys to a mental duel using head games and sexual teasers to manipulate them. Most guys didn't know that they were being played.

Billie Jo was, *"Foot Loose And Fancy Free."* She wasn't afraid to try new things and do things that were considered "Taboo." That was the path that led to her eventual downfall. She had no ears to hear the sounds of danger and no eyes to see what lie ahead.

I prayed a lot for her but my walk with the Lord had a lot

to be desired. I never knew if God ever heard me or even cared. But I prayed anyway.

One night we were driving down a dark country road when a speeding truck hit us head on. Our car spun off the truck and ended in a cornfield. Billie Jo said to me, did you see that guy? I said, what guy? She said, the guy in the white suit. He jumped right in front of us and pushed the car towards the cornfield. We were going to crash head on with that truck but we didn't. I guess nobody saw him but me. As quickly as he appeared, he vanished into the night without a trace."

Michael continues, "I know that we encountered an angel but she would not acknowledge it." She just kelp saying, "that was crazy, Huh?"

"Billie Jo was just 15-years old when she ran away with the bandleader of a "Nowhere" Band. She sent me a letter soon after asking me to tell her mother that she was all right. She said, "I got my man and we're going from bar to bar across country. We're going to make it big."

She was with a "Nowhere Guy", in a "Nowhere Band", in one "Nowhere Bar" after another but I guess that was ok for her because nowhere was "Somewhere" she hadn't been before.

"I was Billie Jo's best friend and she knew that I would not share anything unless she said it was ok. However, I couldn't but wonder if all was really well with her."

"Her handwriting was not the best and her thoughts seemed scattered. They were not clearly expressed. This was unusual for Billie Jo. She was an expert at language and always made an "A" in English class."

"She saw the Mysterious Stranger save our lives that night in the country but took no thought of why. I tried to talk to her about settling down but she wouldn't hear of it."

As Billie Jo and her new found lover went from "Nowhere Bar" to "Nowhere Bar", I realized that she was on the road again in search of that illusive butterfly that was forever out of reach. She could see it but not catch hold of it. It was that inner peace that we all strive to attain. She couldn't settle down because she had no peace inside. She was running away from the chaos and confusion.

Soon the bar hopping got old and the drugs ran out. Yeah, Billie Jo was a slave to cocaine, thanks to her "Nowhere" band leader. He left her in a shabby roadside motel in Indiana with no drugs, no money and pregnant.

As usual, when Billie Jo was in trouble or needed help, she turned to the only friend she ever had, me. I received a call around 2:00 a.m. from a voice crying in the wilderness. "Please help me", she said. "I need you now more than ever."

The drug problem had only worsened over the years. Billie Jo became a drug addict and user of both cocaine and a derivative called crack. It was a party drug and some of the cool movie stars and popular kids liked it. However, its affect on America was devastating. Over 70,000 drug induced deaths occurred in 2017 alone.

Crack cocaine causes weight loss, high blood pressure, hallucinations, seizures, and paranoia. Emergency room visits due to cocaine incidents such as overdoses, unexpected reactions, suicide attempts, and other chronic effects more than doubled.

"So I went to Indiana and rescued Billie Jo. But I never gave her drugs. She went right into a rehab center that I paid for in full until she was better. It took six long and terrible months with daily counseling, special medication and most of all the Word of God."

"The rehab center was run by a Christian organization that believed in the Bible as the inspired word of God. They said that she could be delivered from her drug habit and set free from its residual effects. All she had to do was believe it and hang on to God's Word. That would prove to be extremely difficult for Billie Jo because she was Jewish and turned away at the name of Jesus."

"I took Billie Jo to this rehab because I was raised as a "P. K." That is short for "Pastor's Kid." I grew up hearing the Word of God and being individually taught by my dad. I knew that the only real cure was God and the only inner peace Billie Jo would ever find had to come from Him."

"But it was all up to Billie Jo. She had to be onboard and fight for her soul in the power of the Holy Spirit. Man's psychological counseling would not be enough. She had to put her faith in Jesus and call upon His power to be set free.”

“Back then, I watched many a repentant soul come to Christ but was myself, standoffish. I walked the walk because my dad was the pastor and I talked the talk so I could fit in. However, I had the same void in my heart as Billie Jo had in hers. We both were searching for inner peace.”

“So Billie Jo was dried out, encouraged and sent on her way. She was drug free at least for the moment. However, she lost the baby due to the drugs and stress of trying to get enough money for her next fix. She had a miscarriage.”

“On one hand, she was glad because of the increase of responsibility facing her and her poor parenting skills. She didn’t feel up to caring for a baby when she hardly could care for herself. On the other hand, she was deeply depressed because she felt a sense of relief that her unborn child died.”

“She concluded that God was mad at her and punished her for her drug addiction and immorality. She and I had many talks about a lot of things. Sometimes I got through to her but most of the time she cried too much and couldn’t hear what I was saying.”

I loved Billie Jo. She was my heartthrob since the 10th grade and I knew that God loved her too. It made me sad to think that Billie Jo couldn’t see my love or God’s love.

It was if some evil force blinded her eyes. I knew that it was most likely the drugs that kept her in the dark."

"Well, the long and the short of the story is that Billie Jo fled the scene. She ran as fast as she could in search of that inner peace. She also ran away from God and my love. My heart was stuck on her but her heart was stuck on a habit she just couldn't kick. She thought it would fill the void in her life and bring her peace. Instead it enslaved her and drove her to the brink of insanity."

"About six months later I received a letter from Billie Jo. She was singing in a small nightclub in New Your City. She found another "Nowhere" guy to live with and she kept him in drugs as he was out of work and out of cash."

"Times were hard but she said she was happy. I didn't believe her because I knew that her search for inner peace could only be found in the Lord. She needed to find herself in God to be truly free."

"Telling Billie Jo about God and how He could help brought me again to the realization that I needed the same inner peace, P.K. or not. We both had a void in our souls. She filled it with drugs. I tried to fill it with Billie Jo."

"My dad always said that each person has a void in his or her heart that can only be filled with the love of God. People try to fill it with all sorts of things, thinking that in doing so they will attain happiness and peace of mind. But, as my dad said, "Only God can fill the void in man's soul." It was put there by Him and is exclusively for His indwelling Spirit."

"I shared all of this with Billie Jo in a letter but she never responded back to me. Oh, we talked about other stuff but never again about filling that void."

"Then I received a special delivery letter from Billie Jo. She had miraculously found the Lord and wanted to tell me all about it. As it seemed, she had another visit from that Mysterious Stranger. It was late at night. She was crying and pleading with God to take her life. She said that death would be better that the torment of her life on earth. She sat on the floor with her head in her hands crying and sobbing for hours. Then she heard footsteps as though some intruder was in her small apartment. Then she began to hallucinate, seeing the stars in space speeding by her door and finally settling her on a grassy hill near an old oak tree."

"The footsteps continued until reaching her. She couldn't distinguish reality anymore. Was this an hallucination or was this real? Is it the drugs playing games with my mind or is it God communicating with her?"

"The Mysterious Stranger spoke to Billie Jo and said that it was time for her to choose life or death. He said that both were eternal. He also said that eternal life is the life of God's only begotten Son and His name is Jesus."

"Should she choose death, as she had all of her life up to

this point, she would end up in a big lake of fire, forever to burn in hell that was prepared for the devil and his angels."

"So Billie Jo gave her heart and life to Jesus. She finally realized that He was her salvation and in Him she would find peace."

"The Mysterious Stranger then disappeared and Billie Jo found herself back in her own apartment. She looked at the clock and saw that six hours has passed."

"Billie Jo was the first "*love of my life*" and why I married so late in life. Oh, I dated many other girls but just didn't feel the same with them as I did with Billie Jo. I was happy that she was all right."

"Billie Jo was lost but God found her and now she had another opportunity to live her life to God's glory. I figured, if God could forgive Billie Jo, He could also forgive me. This was also my chance to be with Billie Jo and attain the inner peace I so desperately wanted. That very night I gave me heart to Jesus."

Jim interrupts, "What ever happened to Billie Jo?"

Michael responds, "Hey Melody? Can you come here for a minute?" As Melody approaches Michael introduces her to Jim saying, "Jim? Meet Billie Jo. We call her Melody because God put a song in her heart when she trusted in Jesus and a melody has come forth from her spirit ever since.

I sent her a ticket to come home to me. We were married that same week and have been together ever since."

The Story of Billie Jo was a journey through drugs and immorality that pulled her down to the depths of despair. But it was also the journey of a God-Seeker that found peace of mind and love in this world.

> It's like the Bible says, *"For God so loved the world, that he gave his only begotten Son, that whosoever believes in him should not perish, but have everlasting life."* **John 3:16**

"The story of Billie Jo was also my story. We both suffered under false assumptions of what inner peace was all about and we both felt the pain and anguish of life's many trials. However, God didn't abandon us. He saw to it that we knew the path to His love and grace."

Life is full of Mysteries and Miracles. They come and go through our every days as a train whistling down an old railroad track. The beauty of it all is that we can rest assured that God is with us and that He is working everything, both good and bad, together for our good, so we ultimately benefit from them all. He even sends us His ministering angels to help us along the way.

Well that's my story and I am sticking to it. My heart is full, my life is blessed and my prayers are answered… and above all, my wife loves me. I give thanks to God for making it happen."

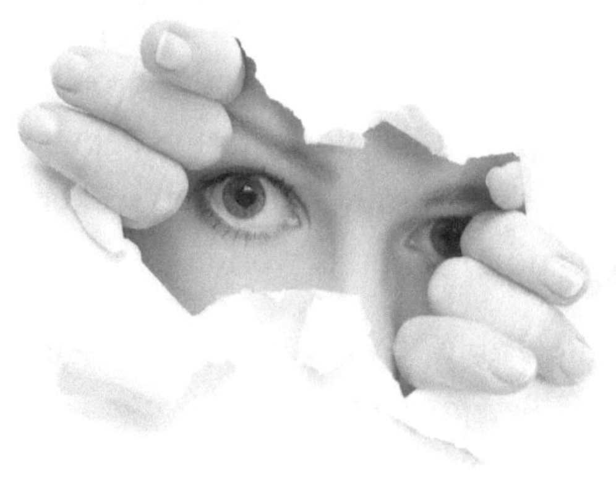

"For God so loved the world, that he gave his only begotten Son, that whosoever believes in him should not perish, but have everlasting life." **John 3:16**

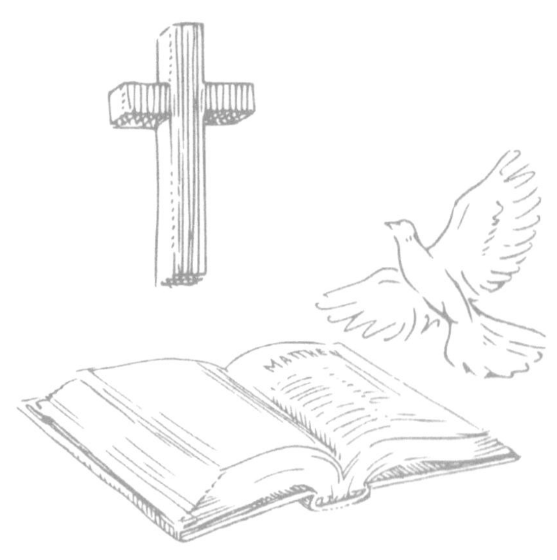

CHAPTER SIXTEEN
WAYS ANGELS MINISTER

Provisions…"*The Lord uses His angels to physically provide for His children. It was an angel who brought Elijah bread and water while fleeing from Jezebel after his victory on Mt. Carmel.*" **1 Kings 19:5-6**

Guidance… "*But while he thought on these things, behold, the angel of the LORD appeared unto him in a dream, saying, Joseph, thou son of David, fear not to take unto thee Mary thy wife: for that which is conceived in her is of the Holy Ghost. And she shall bring forth a son, and thou shalt call his name JESUS: for he shall save his people from their sins.*" **Matthew 1:20-21**

Encouragement… "*And now I exhort you to be of good cheer: for there shall be no loss of any man's life among you, but of the ship. For there stood by me this night the angel of God, whose I am, and* *whom I serve, Saying, Fear not, Paul; thou must be brought before Caesar: and, lo, God hath given thee all them that sail with thee."* **Acts 27:22-24**

Protection... *"My God hath sent his angel, and hath shut the lions' mouths, that they have not hurt me."* **Daniel 6:23**

Rescue or Deliverance... *"And when Herod would have brought him forth, the same night Peter was sleeping between two soldiers, bound with two chains: and the keepers before the door kept the prison. And, behold, the angel of the Lord came upon him, and a light shined in the prison: and he smote Peter on the side, and raised him up, saying, arise up quickly.*

And his chains fell off from his hands. And the angel said unto him, Gird thyself, and bind on thy sandals. And so he did. And he saith unto him, Cast thy garment about thee, and follow me. And he went out, and followed him; and wist not that it was true which was done by the angel; but thought he saw a vision.

When they were past the first and the second ward, they came unto the iron gate that leads unto the city; which opened to them of his own accord: and they went out, and passed on through one street; and forthwith the angel departed from him. And when Peter was come to himself, he said, now I know of a surety, that the Lord hath sent his angel, and hath delivered me out of the hand of Herod, and from all the expectation of the people of the Jews. **Acts 12:6-11**

Healing… *"Then saith Jesus unto him, Get thee hence, Satan: for it is written, Thou shalt worship the Lord thy God, and him only shalt thou serve. Then the devil left him, and, behold, angels came and ministered unto him."* **Matthew 4:10-11**

Also in the garden, *" An angel came from heaven to strengthen him."*

During his agony as he prayed, *"his sweat was as it were great drops of blood falling down upon the ground".* **Luke 22:44**

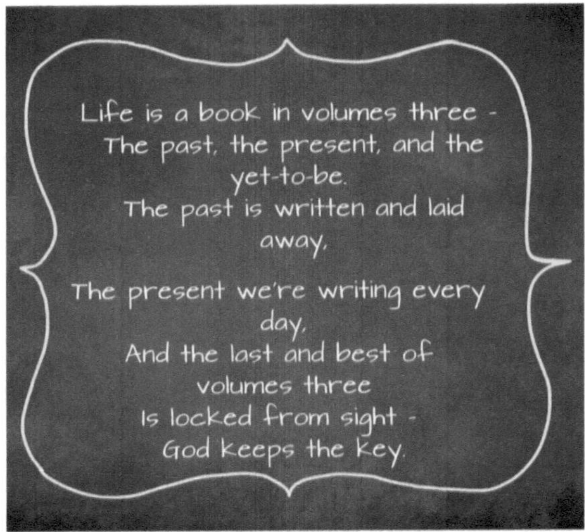

Chapter Seventeen

Questions & Answers

"Wait a minute" Bill, said Jim. "There are still too many questions that are unanswered."

Bill replies, "Like what?"

Jim opens his notebook and begins to read:

1. Do angels have wings?

2. Are there good and bad angels?

3. Is there an army of angels?

4. Do angels communicate with all humans?

5. Are there different types of angels?

6. What do angels do when not tending to our needs?

7. Does everyone have a guardian angel?

Bill again replies to Jim's list of questions saying. "I would stay away from those who speak of angels as though they were his or her next-door neighbors. Lots of folks claim experiences that are self-motivated from an egocentric perspective. Most are a part of the New Age movement that pushes angels and spiritualism. However, we can know about angels because of the Bible.

Angels Are Created Beings. However, there are many misconceptions in today's world. Here are a few common misconceptions that we sometimes may hear but have no bases in Scripture:

1. ***Angels have bodies like human beings***. **False!** Angels, technically, have no physical bodies. Hebrews 1:14 describes them as "ministering spirits." However, God allows them to come in the appearance of man while they are communicating with people on earth.

We get a glimpse of how mighty angels are when Pilot told his best guards to protect the tomb where Jesus was laid. An angel appears and rolls back the stone and the Bible states, "And for fear of him the guards trembled and became like dead men" (Matthew 28:4). Some of the best Roman soldiers could not stand before the grandeur of an angel.

2. ***Angels know all things***. **False!** In Psalm 103, David refers to angels as "mighty ones who do his word." This provides evidence that angels

are strong but are still submissive to God, who is both omnipotent and omniscient. We also know that angels are very wise but not all knowing from Matthew 24:36, where Jesus is talking about the Day of the Lord and He communicates that angels are not aware of when that day will come.

3. ***The only purpose of angels is to protect heaven from evil spirits.*** **False!** This misconception stems from a lack of understanding of the purpose of angels. God uses angels for a variety of purposes. Some angels are ministering spirits that guard and protect God's people (Heb. 1:14, Mark 1:13). Some angels deliver messages from God to humans (Luke 1:26-38, Luke 24:4-7, Rev. 1:1), and many angels ceaselessly worship God in heaven (Rev. 5:11-12).

4. ***Everyone has a guardian angel.*** **False!** There is no convincing evidence in Scripture that every person has their own specific guardian angel. There are angels who protect, guard and minister to God's people (Ps. 91:11-12), but the wicked have no angels of God to protect and guide them. They have only demonic spir-

its that seek to torment them, kill their dreams, steel their peace and destroy their destiny. They often transform themselves into angels of light in an attempt to deceive the elect of God but they are still evil spirits.

I believe in angels because the Bible plainly teaches that they exist. From Genesis to Revelation we read all about them. At least 250 Bible passages speak of angels. The last book of the Bible alone has 80 references. Surely, with so many Scriptures about them, it is a subject worthy of our careful attention.

Both the Hebrew word *mal'ak* and the Greek word *ange-los*, from which we get the word "angel," simply mean "messenger." People often mistook angels for ordinary people, but these heavenly messengers are greater than mortal beings and they are not all alike.

Angels are personal and moral beings. Angels are always portrayed with personal attributes, including intelligence, volition, and a moral nature. Their wisdom and power are vastly superior to our human abilities (2 Sam. 14:20; Ps. 103:20), but their knowledge is by no means exhaustive (there are "things into which angels long to look into," 1 Peter 1:12; as well as facts they do not know, Matt. 24:36).

The angels are a mighty multitude. Without giving

any hint as to their actual number, Scripture makes it clear that the angelic host is a vast and imposing army. The expression "host of heaven," often used to signify the angels (Deut. 4:19; 2 Chron. 18:18; Luke 2:13), suggests an innumerable throng (see Jer. 33:22).

The angels were apparently created all at once, yet individually. They are never portrayed as a race descended from a common ancestor (Luke 20:34–36). Humans are called "sons of men," but angels are never called "sons of angels." As a matter of fact, Jesus emphatically said that angels do not marry (Matt. 22:30). As to gender, they are always referred to with masculine pronouns — but since they have no feminine counterparts and are spiritual beings who do not procreate, it would seem that they cannot meaningfully be categorized as either male or female.

But they are nonetheless organized in ranks and legions similar to a massive army. Again, the expression "host of heaven" evokes the idea of an armed company. Jesus said on the night of His betrayal that he could have instantly summoned "more than twelve legions of angels" to fight on His behalf (Matt. 26:53).

The orders of angels are not fully enumerated or explained by the Bible. But the angelic host includes at least one archangel, the seraphim, and the cherubim. The archangel, Michael, is named in Daniel 10:13, 21; Jude 9; and Revelation 12:7. He seems to be the highest of all angelic creatures. Only one other holy angel, Gabriel, is explicitly named (Dan. 8:16; 9:21; Luke 1:19, 26). Some think he is therefore similar in rank to Michael, but Scripture doesn't actually designate Gabriel as an archangel.

> *Angels are God's unseen ministers.* One of the most interesting questions of all about angels has to do with their unseen service on behalf of believers. Scripture portrays angels as caretakers of God's providence on our behalf — "ministering spirits sent out to serve for the sake of those who are to inherit salvation" (Heb. 1:14). In Matthew 18:10, Jesus (speaking of His own tender care for little children) said, "I tell you that in heaven their angels always see the face of my Father who is in heaven" — suggesting that specific angels have guardianship of specific individuals.

The Bible tells us that there are Three Functional Categories of Angels.

> **Warring Angels**…This includes the great army of angels that stand at the gates of heaven, at the gates of hell and stand ready to deliver the saints from harm.

> **Ministering Spirits** that are caretakers of God's providence and ministers to those who will inherit salvation.

> **Angels of Worship** that praise God before His throne day and night.

Jim interrupts Bill with more questions and Bill continues to explain.

Can We Communicate With Angels?…The Bible does not support human beings ever contacting angels. It does, however, support angels talking to humans. They are messengers from God.

Do Angels Marry Each Other?… For in the resurrection they (people) neither marry, nor are given in marriage, but are as the angels of God in heaven." **Matthew 22:30**

Was Satan An Angel?… The Bible nowhere explicitly describes Satan as an angel before he rebelled against God and was cast out of heaven. Assuming Ezekiel 28:12–18 is symbolic of Satan's fall, Satan is described as a "guardian cherub." Cherubs are angelic creatures, possibly the highest order of angels. So, in that sense, yes, Satan was an angel.

Are Fallen Angels Demons?… When exactly God created angels is open for debate, but what is known for sure is that God created everything good because God, in His holiness, cannot create something sinful. So when Satan, who was once the angel, Lucifer, rebelled against God and fell from heaven (Isaiah 14; Ezekiel 28), one third of the angelic host joined his insurrection (Revelation 12:3-4,9). There is no doubt these fallen angels are now known as demons.

Where Do Evil Angels Get Their Power?…The Bible declares that Christ utterly defeated Satan, "And having spoiled principalities and powers, he made a shew of them openly, triumphing over them in it." **Colossians 2:15**

Thus Jesus stripped all evil forces of their power. The only power they have now is the power we give them from our free will choices. That's why we are to resist, stand in faith and give no place to the devil.

Can Or Did Angels Intermarry With Human Beings?... Nowhere in the Scriptures does it say that these "sons of God" spoken of in Genesis are angels. Also, if you look at the context of Genesis 6; Genesis 5 is talking about Adam's lineage. In chapter 5, the phrase that is repeated constantly is that Adam's descendants "begat sons". Or "begat sons and daughters". So, according to the context, these "sons of God" are humans. If you turn to Deuteronomy 14:1, this also proves that the "sons of God" are actually humans. Plus, as we have seen already, angels are unable to procreate. In the resurrection, we will be like them, without sexual desires or abilities.

Is God An Angel?... God is a triune being. He has no beginning or end. He always was and always is. He is the creator of all that exists. He is not an angel.

Can Angels Harm Humans... Yes they can but usually do not. There is an example in the bible where angels blinded some of the men of Sodom who wanted to abuse the angels that were in Lot's house. **Genesis 19.** There was also a time where Jacob was touched by an angel when he was wrestling with him and was hurt. **Genesis 32:22-32**

Do Angels Die?... Angels do not die because they were originally created as spirit beings. They are eternal. **Luke 20:36** However, this is in the traditional sense meaning as a human would stop breathing and die. There is another meaning for death that says, death is the eternal separation from God. The being does not cease to exist. It does however exist in total darkness, separated from God and alone. We call this place Hell.

Are Angels Male Or Female?... There is no doubt that every reference to angels in Scripture is in the masculine gender. The Greek word for "angel" in the New Testament, *angelos*, is in the masculine form. In fact, a feminine form of *angelos* does not exist. There are three genders in grammar—masculine (*he, him, his*), feminine (*she, her, hers*), and neuter (*it, its*). Angels are never referred to in any gender other than masculine. In the many appearances of angels in the Bible, never is an angel referred to as "she" or "it." Furthermore, when angels appeared, they were always dressed as human males (Genesis 18:2, 16; Ezekiel 9:2). No angel ever appears in Scripture dressed as a female.

The angels in Revelation are all spoken of as "he" and their possessions as "his" (Revelation 10:1, 5; 14:19; 16:2, 4, 17; 19:17; 20:1). However, the masculine gender pronouns applied to spirit beings are more a reference to authority than to sex.

What Do Angels Look Like?... Angels are spirit beings (Hebrews 1:14), so they do not have any essential physical form. But angels do have the ability to appear in human form. When angels appeared to humans in the Bible, they resembled normal males.

In Genesis 18:1-19, God and two angels appeared as men and actually ate a meal with Abraham. Angels appear as men many times throughout the Bible (Joshua 5:13-14; Mark 16:5), and they never appear in the likeness of women.

Other times, angels appeared not as humans, but as something other-worldly, and their appearance was terrifying to those who encountered them. Often, the first words from these angels were "do not be afraid," because extreme fear was such a common reaction. The keepers of Jesus' tomb became as dead men when they saw the angel of the Lord (Matthew 28:4). The shepherds in the fields in Luke 2 were "sore afraid" when the angel of the Lord appeared and the glory of the Lord shone around them.

As for physical characteristics, angels are sometimes described as winged. The images of cherubim on the ark of the covenant had wings that covered the mercy seat (Exodus 25:20). Isaiah saw winged seraphim in his vision of the throne of heaven, each one having six wings (Isaiah 6:2). Ezekiel, too, saw visions of winged angels. Isaiah 6:1-2 depicts angels having human features—voices, faces and feet. Angel voices are heard singing and praising God in several other passages. The angel at Jesus' tomb is described as having a brilliant appearance: "His countenance was like lightning, and his raiment white as snow" (Matthew 28:3).

Whatever appearance angels take on, there is reason to believe they are incredibly beautiful. Ezekiel tells us that Lucifer was "lifted up" in pride over his beauty. In addition, beings such as angels, who are continually in the presence of God, would be expected to have extraordinary beauty because God's glory is reflected upon all that is around Him

Why Did Some Angels Rebel Against God?... Most theologians believe that Lucifer's cry to replace God with himself is recorded in the bible, "I will ascend above the heights of the clouds; I will be like the most High. **Isaiah 14:14**. His bid for the throne of God was why 1/3 of all the angels followed him in a war that was waged in heaven and where he lost and all of them were thrown out.

Do We Become Angels When We Die? Angels are beings created by God (Colossians 1:15-17) and are entirely different from humans. They are God's special agents to carry out His plan and to minister to the followers of Christ (Hebrews 1:13-14). There is no indication that angels were formerly humans or anything else—they were created as angels. Angels have no need of, and cannot experience, the redemption that Christ came to provide for the human race.

First Peter 1:12 describes their desire to look into the Gospel, but it is not for them to experience. Had they been formerly humans, the concept of salvation would not be a mystery to them, having experienced it themselves. Yes, they rejoice when a sinner turns to Christ (Luke 15:10), but salvation in Christ is not for them.

Jim replied to everything that Bill said. "Thanks for the Bible study. It is a good thing to know that God's ministering spirits are active in the earth. Much of what they do goes un-noticed except by those that have an encounter with a mysterious Stranger. They know that God is looking out for them."

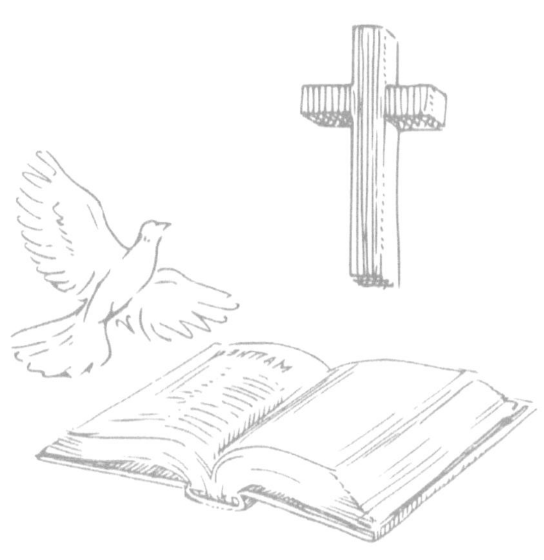

CONCLUSION

Life is full of Mysteries and Miracles. They come and go through our every days as a train whistling down an old railroad track. The beauty of it all is that we can rest assured that God is with us and He is working everything, both good and bad, together for our good, so we ultimately benefit from them all. He even sends us His ministering angels to help us along the way to Glory.

We are not alone in this life. He is with us and His love is all around us. Just knowing Him brings us inner peace.

Well that's my story. My heart is full, my life is blessed and my prayers are answered…and above all, my wife loves me. I give thanks to God for making it all happen.

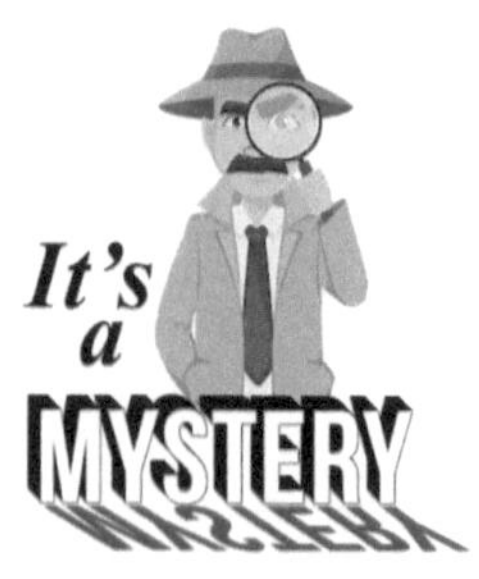

ABOUT THE AUTHOR

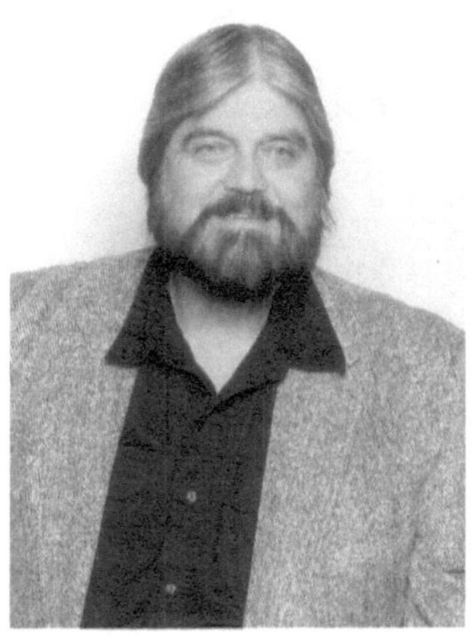

John Marinelli

Rev. Marinelli is an ordained minister, He has formed and been pastor of one church in Wisconsin and was the pastor of another in Alabama. He has also been a youth minister and evangelism director over the years.

Rev. Marinelli has authored several books including: "Original Story Poems", a children's story poem book", "The Art of Writing Christian Poetry," "Pulpit Poems," "Mysteries & Miracles" a Christian Fiction story, "Moonlight & Mistletoe" Another Christian Fiction book and many others.

He is also the author of over 80 eBooks on various Christian subjects. They are all free downloads from his website;

www.christianliferesourcecenter.org

John is an accomplished Christian poet. He also dabbles in songwriting and writing one act Christian plays.

He is the Vice President of Have A Heart For Companion Animals, Inc., a "No Kill" animal welfare organization.

www.haveaheart.us

John is now retired and living in sunny Florida. He enjoys writing, chess, karaoke and sharing Jesus with whoever will listen.

Rev. Marinelli is now retired from the sales and marketing arena after spending over 40 years in business-to-business and non-profit marketing.

Rev. Marinelli enjoys writing Christian fiction stories, playing chess, singing karaoke and a retired lifestyle in sunny Florida.

Quiet Hours

In the silence of the quiet hours
In the presence of a new dawn,
I bow down upon my knees,
For bringing me life reborn

Taking off all the shackles,
Letting my spirit free.
I give all the thanks to Jesus,
For giving His love to me.

Written By Marilyn Marinelli

THE ANGELS CRY HOLY

The Angels cry "Holy,"
While sorrow fills the land.
For God's Judgment Day,
Is to come upon every man.

The Angels cry "Holy,"
While mankind goes astray,
Rejecting the love of God,
To follow his own precarious way.

The Angels cry "Holy,"
Knowing the terror of the Lord,
When all who dwell in sin,
Will suddenly be destroyed.

The Angels cry "Holy,"
Waiting for all things new,
Born of the Holy Spirit,
When God's Judgment is through.

The Angels cry "Holy,"
"Holy is the Lamb,"
Waiting for the children of God,
To join "The Great I AM"

"And one cried unto another and said, "Holy, Holy, Holy, is the Lord of host: the whole earth is full of his glory" Isaiah 6:3

We serve a Holy God that deserves our reverence and homage. The angels know this and worship Him, but man, because of sin, has no real concept of his own creator.

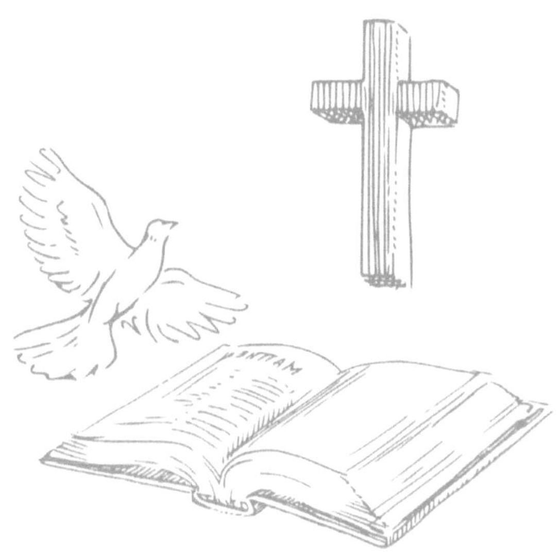

My Guardian Angel

The angel of the Lord
Comes with a mighty army,
To fight the enemies of God.

Then he opens our eyes
That we might see the battle
And walk where angels trod.

Our guardian angels
Beholds the very face of God,
Standing there on our behalf.

Our guardian angels
Are ready with God's power,
To quiet evil's awful wrath.

"Take heed that ye despise not one of these little ones; for I say unto you, That in heaven, there angels do always behold the face of my Father, which is in heaven" Mathew 18:10

As God's children, we have guardian angels that watch over us and report back to God. They are ministering spirits especially placed in service to help the saints on their way to glory.

THE ANGEL'S CAMP

The angel of the Lord
Sets up his camp
Around those that reverence God.

Imagine being there
In the midst of
Where angels trod.

What a joy it is
To know God's protection
And to be in the angel's camp.

It is there that God's children
Are delivered from evil's woe
And led by heaven's lamp.

"The angel of the Lord encamps round about them that fear Him, and delivers them" Psalm 34:7

Deliverance come through reverence and respect for God and a belief that He will be there with His angels to help you in times of trouble.